SIMCHAH
THE SPARK OF LIFE

SIMCHAH
The Spark of Life

A comprehensive exploration of the
virtue of Simchah: "Jewish Happiness"
and how to attain it.

by

Rabbi Alexander Aryeh Mandelbaum

First published 1995

ISBN 0-87306-732-0

Edited by Shalom Kaplan

Distributed by:
FELDHEIM PUBLISHERS
POB 35002   200 Airport Executive Park
Jerusalem, Israel   Nanuet, NY 10954

Printed in Israel

"Simchah is the spark of life, the spark which ignites our ambition to rise to the heights of self-fulfillment and success. It is the driving force behind all human development from the very first moment of life."(p. 116)

In memory of our beloved parents

ר׳ ישראל בן ר׳ דוד ז״ל

ע״ה **Israel Weiss**

and

נעמי בת שבע בת הרב ברוך יוסף ז״ל

ע״ה **Naomi Twersky**

*By filling their lives with true Torah values
they have left a legacy of simcha for their
children and grandchildren -
"...the source of the Simcha of eternity."*

Dr. & Mrs. David Weiss

TABLE OF CONTENTS

הרב לוי יצחק הלוי הורוויץ

דער באסטאנער רבי

Grand Rabbi Levi Y. Horowitz

מוסדות בוסטון בארה״ק
בנשיאות האדמו״ר שליט״א
מעלות האדמו״ר מבוסטון ז
הר נוף, ירושלים Israel

ב״ה

BOSTONER REBBE
RABBI LEVI YITZCHAK HOROWOITZ

I was pleased to learn that Rabbi Alexander Aryeh Mandelbaum Shlita is about to publish a Sefer entitled Simchah - the Spark of Life (an English version of his Hebrew work V'hoyiso Ach Someach) - a comprehensive exploration of the virtue of Simchah, which is the foundation of Chassidut and the source of true Jewish life.

This work is very important especially in our time, when - although we were merited to see the growth and flourishing of the Jewish people in general and the expansion of Torah institutions in particular, to an extent unparallelled since the days of Chazal - yet there are problems characteristic of our modern era which at times cause people to be in a state of depression. This is specially evident after the dreadful Holocaust, and there is a dire need for S'forim of this nature by people with the talent of Chizuk to help them maintain the state of Simchah.

The book is well-structured and written in a logical, step-by-step build-up, easily followed. It was adapted in a manner that both the beginner and the advanced Torah student can benefit from it.

I, therefore, wholeheartedly endorse this Sefer that has already made a powerful impact upon thousands of Hebrew readers, and extend my blessing to the young author that he should be Zocheh to further inspire the English-speaking public with the Spark of Life.

Levi Yitzchak Horowitz
(Grand Rabbi of Boston)

Approbation given for the Hebrew *sefer V`Hayita Ach Sameach* by Rabbi **Shlomo Wolbe** *Shlit"a*, **Beit HaMussar**, Jerusalem

הר"ר שלמה וולבה שליט"א
בית המוסר ירושלים

מכתב תודה

לכבוד ידידי הנעלה הרב ר' אלכסנדר מנדלבאום שליט"א

שלום וברכה מרובה!

הנני מחכה להופעת ספרו הנכבד "והיית אך שמח", כי בוודאי הוא יהי' לתועלת מרובה עבורי ועבור רבים כמוני לתת שמחה בלבנו.

עיקר כה גדול הוא "עבדו את ה' בשמחה" - ומה דלים חיינו כהיום בשמחה אמיתית ועמוקה בתורתו ובמצוותיו ית'. לא כך ראינו אצל רבותינו הגדולים זי"ע אשר חייהם היו מלאי שמחה ועונג: שמחה בתורתם, עונג בשבתותיהם, שמחה בתפילתם ושמחה בחלקם - וכמה רחוקים אנחנו היום מכל זה.

יהי רצון שתתגלגל זכות הרבים על ידי כתי"ר לעוררנו על השמחה בהיותנו עובדי השי"ת ומקיימי מצוותיו, ובזה יהי' ממזכי הרבים ככוכבים לעולם ועד!

ברוב הוקרה וכבוד
שלמה וולבה

ט"ז תמוז תשמ"ט

Approbation given for the Hebrew *sefer V`Hayita Ach Sameach* from the **GERER REBBE** *SHLIT"A* (Grand Rabbi of Gur) Rabbi **Pinchas Menachem Alter**, Jerusalem

כ"ק האדמו"ר מגור
הרב פינחס מנחם אלטר שליט"א
בהרה"ק מגור זצללה"ה

בה"יי, י"ז ימים לחדש שיהפך בה"יי מיגון לשמחה ומאבל לי"ט תשמ"ט, פעה"ק ירושלם תובב"יא.

לכב' הר"יר אלכסנדר מנדלבוים שליט"א, מתלמידי ישיבת מיר, כאן.

ראיתי את חיבורו "והיית אך שמח", ועברתי על מקצתו, וכידוע אנני נותן הסכמות באופן עקרוני, אבל גם א"יי למה צריך להסכמתי אחרי שייל כבר הסכמות מגדולי תורה זצ"יל הקודמים ומראשי ישיבות שליט"א יבדלחט"א כעת.

והחיבור עצמו אם יביא לשמחה של מצוה - תורה - שמחה של קדושה - לשמוח במעלות ישראל, ובעיקר שמחה בעבודת השי"ת שציוונו וזכינו לעשות רצונו, הוא דבר חשוב, ובפרט כעת כאשר העצבות גדולה.

והנני מברכו שיצליח בה"יי להפיץ עי"יז שמחה של מצוה.

פנחס מנחם אלטר

Approbation given for the Hebrew *sefer V`Hayita Ach Sameach* by Rabbi **Ovadia Yossef** *Shlit"a*
Richon Lezion - Chief Rabbi of Israel

OVADIA YOSSEF

RICHON LEZION CHIEF RABBI OF ISRAEL

עובדיה יוסף

ראשון לציון הרב הראשי לישראל

בעה ירושלים _____ JERUSALEM

שנת ,,והיית אך שמח" ה'תשנ"א לפ"ק

(הסכמה)

הובאו לפני גליונות ספר ,,והיית אך שמח" אשר ידי אמוני וסופר נאמן
המחבר הריל ומי אשתו בן ונעי רבי אלכסנדר אניתלביתס שליט"א.
ענינ האאחה, ומקורות ואמונע מיוסדים על אבני סל, דרוכים
כטור עם ובזאת תקותי כתב באמונית כמל דבר דבור על אופנו.
עול ברם אאחי ונרח שמנק ונפט ואמרא ואצם.

ויהי רצון שיפק ה' כיבו יצלח למחך על האומאר וסיבינו אמינואת
מלאה להאיל תקונה להמיבינה במות הותורה את פ שו
ווצוה. והיה כרף שלל אל פלגי מימ אשר פריו יתן בעתן
ועלהו לא יבול ובל אשר יעה יצליח.

בברכת התורה

עובדיה יוספ

Approbation given for the Hebrew *sefer V`Hayita Ach Sameach* by Rabbi **Moshe Halberstam** *Shlit"a,* Motz Eidah HaCharedit, Rosh Yeshiva **Divrei Chaim** Jerusalem

הרב משה הלברשטאם שליט"א
מו"צ בהעדה החרדית
ראש ישיבת "דברי חיים" טשאקאווע
פעיה"ק ירושלים תובב"א

בס"ד, דבר טוב ויפה הגה ברוחו הטהור חד מבני ציון היקרים, ה"ר
האברך כפשוטו ומדרשו, המו"מ בתוי"ש שקדן וגריס באורייתא
בתדירא, ממשפחת אפרתים כש"ת מוהר"ר אלכסנדר מנדלבום
שליט"א מחשובי הלומדים בישיבה הגדולה והקדושה דמיר בפעיה"ק
ת"ו. אשר לקח לו עתו ועטו בידו לעורר את הלבבות, לאחד מיסודי
ועיקרי תורה"ק, והם לקיים מצוות הבוי"ת בשמחה, ולהיות בשמחה
תמיד וכמאמר דוד המלך: עבדו את ה' בשמחה וגו' (תהילים ק').
ומקרא מלא מפורש בתורה על מי שלא נזהר בזה "תחת אשר לא עבדת
את ה"א בשמחה וגו'" (דברים כ"ח מ"ז). והצליח המחבר הה"ג
שליט"א ללקט ולאסוף דברים המתקבלים על הלב מדברי חז"ל
וראשונים ומפי סופרים וספרים. ועלתה בידו חיבור נאה ויאה אשר
בשם "והיית אך שמח" קראוהו. וגם הוסיף בו דברים ערבים בשבח
מדותיו של אדם ולהעיר ולהאיר בדרך הטוב והישר בעיני א' ואדם.
וכוונתו ופעולתו של הה"ג המחבר שליט"א טובה ורצויה מאד, לתת
השמחה והערבות בלבו של אדם, נר ה' נשמת אדם, ולהיות שמח
בחלקו שנתן לו הקב"ה, ושם חלקנו בתורתו. ואשרי מי שעמלו בתורה,
ואמינא לפעלא טבא יישר. וכדאי והגון ונכון להוציאו לאור עולם
ולזכות בזה את הרבים ובכלל מזכה הרבים יחשב. ויזכה להפיץ
מעיינותיו חוצה להגדיל תורה ולהאדירה, עדי נזכה כולנו לשמחת עולם
על ראשנו, וששון ושמחה ישיגו ונס יגון ואנחה, בבוא לציון גואל
במהרה.

ובעה"ח היום יום ד', ו' לחודש הרחמים והסליחות. יומא הילולא רבא
של כ"ק זקני הגה"ק מחי"ס ייטב לב זי"ע, שנת "ישמח לבב אנוש"
לפ"ק.

משה הלברשטאם
עבד לעבדי ה' בקהלא קדישא
דבירושלים תובב"א

Approbation given for the Hebrew *sefer V`Hayita Ach Sameach* by Rabbi **Aryeh Leib Finkel** *Shlit"a* Rosh Yeshiva **Mir**, Jerusalem

הרב הגאון ר' אריה לייב פינקל שליט"א
ר"מ בישיבת מיר, ירושלים

לכבוד ידי"נ הרב המופלג בתוי"ש אברך כמדרשו, אחד המיוחדים מחובשי בית מדרשנו, מוה"ר אלכסנדר מנדלבוים שליט"א.

אתך החיים והשלום

ברגשי כבוד הנני לאשר קבלת הגליונות של ספרך הנפלא "והיית אך שמח". והנה יום הופעת ספרך הוא יום שמחה למעיינים ולצמאים לדבר ה'. ועיקר מעלת הספר באשר הוא שווה לכל נפש, גם צעירי הלומדים ירוון וישאבו ממנו מלא נפש נחת, גם הגדולים וחקרי לב ירחב וירהב לבבם למראה הדברים המאירים והשמחים כנתינתן מסיני.

יה"ר שיפוצו מעיינותיך בי מדרשא ויהיו בוודאי לתועלת עצומה לכל בן תורה בכל אתר ואתר.

ידידך עז מוקירך ומכבדך
בכל לב

ארי' ליב פינקל

Approbation given for the Hebrew *sefer VeSamachta*
B`eChagecha by Rabbi **Chaim P. Scheinberg** *Shlit"a*
Kiryat Mattersdorf, Rosh Yeshiva "**Torah Or**", Jerusalem

הרב הגאון הרב חיים פינחס שיינברג שליט"א
ראש ישיבת "תורה אור"
ומורה הוראה דקרית מטרסדורף

בעזהי"ת, סיון תשנ"א

מכתב תהילה

להרב ר' אלכסנדר מנדלבוים שליט"א, אשר הביא לפני גליונות מספרו
"ושמחת בחגך", להעיר ולעורר הלבבות בענין העומד ברומו של עולם,
והבריות דשין בו בעקבם - השמחה במועדים.

הגם שאין דרכי לתת הסכמה לשום ספר, אך דברי שבח ותהילה על
התועלת של הספר הסכמתי.

ספר זה הוא אוצר בלום מפי ספרים וסופרים המדבר אודות המשמעות
הפנימית של המועדים, ועוד הוסיף המחבר נופך משלו להאיר ולבאר
הרבה מאמרי חז"ל העמוקים. הספר נכתב בסגנון מיוחד לעורר את
האדם לחוש מהרוממות ומהקדושה של המועדים.

וכבר אתמחי גברא בספרו הראשון "והיית אך שמח", הנודע בשערים,
המדבר על מעלת השמחה בעבודת השי"ת.

והריני מברכו שיפוצו מעיינותיו חוצה, וישתו רבים בצמא דבריו
המאירים והמשמחים.

**הכותב והחותם למען התורה
ולומדיה**

חיים פינחס שיינברג

Note To The Reader

We have made special efforts to adapt our *sefer* — *V'hay-ita Ach Sameach* — in a way that can be understood at all levels. When a source from the N'viim (Prophets) is quoted or made reference to, the name of the source appears in Latin, so as to make it easier for the beginner.

Commonly known Torah sources are transliterated and written in italics.

All other Hebrew transliterated words are italicized, with the exception of well-known words, such as Simchah; Hashem; Midrash; Yeshiva; Torah; Mitzvah.

ACKNOWLEDGEMENTS

Having completed this work, the translation and adaptation of my first *sefer, V'Hayita Ach Sameach,* for the English speaking public, it is my sacred obligation to acknowledge those to whom recognition is due.

First and foremost, my rabbis and mentors, HaGaon Rav Chaim Shmulevitz, Ztz"l, and, *Yibadel l'Chayim,* HaGaon Rav Moshe Shapiro, *Shlit"a* — my spiritual fathers who taught me Torah. Much of this work is an interpretation of their teachings, according to my humble ability and meager understanding.

My deepest gratitude is extended to my revered father, *Shlit"a,* "Simcha". His name is most appropriate, as all who are acquainted with him know that he is the central joyful spirit at the Shabbat and Yom Tov meals, at Simchat Torah celebrations, as well as at every Simchah. As a child in our home, I was imbued with his guidance and teachings, and during my formative years I began to take a special interest in the virtue of Simchah, and I developed a desire to explore and understand this wonderful facet of life to the best of my ability. I hope to be able to convey and to kindle the spark of life in the hearts of all who are seeking true happiness. It was only through the support and encouragement of my father and mother that this work has reached fruition. May it be the will of the Almighty that he and my beloved mother, Malka, enjoy a long life of Simchah, good health and *nachas* from all their children and grandchildren.

I wish to extend my deepest appreciation to my father-in-law, Rabbi Aryeh Julius, for editing the Hebrew edition and undertaking the translation of the bulk of the English edition. It is mainly because of his constant support that this book was able to reach completion. May HaShem bless him and his wife, Rachel, with *brachos* and *nachas* from all their children and grandchildren.

In addition, I am deeply indebted to three individuals who worked on large segments of the book: Rabbi Moshe Shapiro, Mrs. M. Steinberger and Mr. Shalom Kaplan, whose questions and comments as editor contributed greatly to clarify the presentation of the more difficult concepts introduced in this book.

I also want to extend my deepest thanks to my mother and to Mrs. Rivka Heimowitz who wholeheartedly volunteered their talents to complete this work. Let HaShem repay them generously for their goodness.

Lastly, I can never adequately express my gratitude to my wife Elkah, about whom the words of Rabbi Akiva to his *talmidim* are most appropriate: "Mine and yours, are hers." May HaShem bless us all with Simchah, *brachah* and *yiddishe nachas*.

PREFACE

Simchah — A Privilege and an Obligation

One of man's greatest drives is the desire to achieve happiness. This intrinsic drive has a very strong influence on a person's life. Let's ask ourselves: Why does a person devote so much energy, time and money to beautify his home? Why does he travel great distances and spend a fortune on hotels, expensive restaurants and other forms of entertainment? Why does he always seek something new, special and different? What is he *really* looking for when he goes out to seek all kinds of distractions and amusements, of which such an abundance exists in our modern-day society? Is it not the driving force of all man's action and creativity under the sun: the pursuit of happiness?

The Torah, the most profound guidebook available for achieving ultimate perfection, does not command us to suppress this drive. On the contrary, it commands us to encourage and even *exalt* these feelings...but through the unique Torah method, as we shall explain later.

Judaism's attitude towards Simchah (happiness) is described by Rabbi Shimshon Rafael Hirsch (*Ma'agalei Hashanah*, Section 2:98): "Judaism never considered pain, sorrow, self-affliction, or sadness to be valid goals. The opposite is true: one should pursue happiness, bliss, cheer, joy, and delight. For the *Shechinah* (Holy Presence) does not dwell in a place of sadness; it dwells only in a place where happiness reigns. The Torah strongly rejects sorrow and sadness. [It] teaches us to live a life permeated with happiness and joy."

Ultimate Perfection

There are those who think that the ultimate perfection of man is to be achieved by living a life of sadness, self-affliction and abstention from physical pleasures. However, the Torah teaches that man should follow the middle path and strive to live a happy life.

The Rambam explains this concept (*Hilchot De'ot* 3:1): "Lest one should conclude, 'Since the negative traits cause man to become uprooted from the world, I will distance myself from them completely — I will not eat meat, drink wine, marry a woman, live in a comfortable home, wear fine clothes....' This is an incorrect path, and it is prohibited to follow it. Accordingly, one who conducts himself in this manner is considered a sinner. For this reason, the Sages discourage abstaining from pleasures which the Torah does not forbid."

Similarly, the Sages say (*Berachot* 57b): "Three things expand man's mind. They are: a comfortable home, a beautiful wife, and many possessions."

Thus, we see that it is in accordance with the spirit of the Torah to remove ourselves from sadness and serve G-d with happiness.

Simchah — A Torah Precept

What is the source in the Torah for the mitzvah of Simchah?

The *mishnah* says (*Pirkei Avot* 4:1): "Who is a wealthy person? He who rejoices with his portion." Concerning this statement, the Rambam writes (*Hilchot De'ot* 2:7): "A person should not be in a constant state of laughter and jest, nor sad and mournful. Instead, one should *be joyful*. In addition, he should not be excessively hard-working, nor overly indulgent. Instead, one should work minimally and study Torah, and *feel content* with his earnings, which is his lot...."

It is apparent from the Rambam that being joyful and happy with one's lot assumes the same importance as other positive character traits such as modesty, piousness, etc. In the beginning of *Hilchot De'ot*, the Rambam writes that it is a mitzvah from the Torah to attain *all* the positive character traits. Thus, it is evident that we are commanded by the Torah to be satisfied with our lives.

Rabbi Yehudah Halevi (*Kuzari* 3:11) is of the opinion that this mitzvah has a more explicit source: "It is not in accordance with the spirit of the Torah to worry and feel anguish throughout one's life; one who does so transgresses the

Almighty's commandment to be content with what he has been granted, as it says (*Devarim* 26:11): 'And you shall rejoice with every good thing which the Lord your G-d has given you and your family, together with the Levite and the stranger who is within your midst.' "

Rabbeinu Yonah, in his commentary to Tractate *Berachot* (*Rif p. 30*), considers unhappiness an illness, of which one must be cured: "There is a beneficial aspect to sadness — it prevents people from becoming overly joyous over the pleasures of this world. However, one *should not pursue* the state of sadness, since it is a physical disease. When a person is despondent, he is not able to serve his Creator properly. One should not be overly joyous nor sad, but rather, travel the middle road between these two extremes."

Thus, we see that although the early Halachic authorities differ regarding the source of the commandment of Simchah, all agree that Simchah is a Torah precept and a worthy trait that one should strive to acquire.

The Aim of This Book

The purpose of this book is to open pathways to Torah-true happiness. We will see that Simchah is an acquired virtue and *anyone* with Torah as his or her guiding force can make it an internalized personality trait.

We will work towards achieving true Simchah via the following steps:

A) Through coming to understand the deeper meaning of the term Simchah.

B) Through delving into the depths of our minds in order to understand how human psychology works.

C) Through blending the theoretical concepts with our own personal feelings.

We will learn how to be *B'Simchah* through several practical approaches, until true happiness has taken root in our hearts and souls. Anyone can come to lead a life steeped in Simchah!

The Structure of This Book

We actually experience Simchah in two ways: The first is "Passive Simchah" — a general feeling of satisfaction and contentment. The second is "Active Simchah" — a positive feeling of cheerfulness and joy, a feeling which produces an elevated spirit. These two types of Simchah are included in the Torah commandment mentioned above — to feel happy with our lives.

Part One of this book deals with Passive Simchah and Part Two with Active Simchah. The third Part then explores the Torah-True Simchah, which paves the way to reaching the ultimate joy: Simchah in Mitzvot and Simchah in HaShem.

PART I

"PASSIVE SIMCHAH":

Satisfaction and Contentment

1

SIMCHAH —
AN ACQUIRED VIRTUE

We noted in the preface, that dispelling feelings of sadness and being happy is a great mitzvah. Rebbi Nachman of Breslav said (*Likutei Moharan Chelek Beit* 24), "It is a great mitzvah to be perpetually happy, and to overcome and reject feelings of sorrow and melancholy."

Orchot Tzaddikim (*Sha'ar* 9) describes the state of complete happiness thus:

> "Happiness is the feeling of complete peace
> in one's heart, without any sense of fear. One
> who achieves his desires and suffers nothing
> which saddens him will be constantly
> happy."

But this description seems like a complete fantasy! Has anyone ever achieved such bliss in this world?

The happiness described in the *Orchot Tzaddikim* can be the possesion of everyone, without exception. But one must first learn what the nature of true happiness is, and the steps one must take to attain it.

Most people equate happiness with a spontaneous reaction to an external occurrence, such as a concert, a special dinner or a wedding. As a result, they are constantly seeking new experiences to elevate their feelings of "joy." In contrast, the happiness which the Torah teaches us to acquire is on a much deeper level.

External experiences have, at most, the power to produce temporary elation. They produce a superficial *feeling* of happiness, but not the internalized *virtue* of happiness itself. For when the joyful event is over, the excitement passes and one reverts to his or her former state.

Technology and automation have helped foster the attitude that things can be accomplished instantly, without self-exertion.

More and more gadgets are designed to do their tasks at the push of a button. One might expect to push a button for turning on feelings of happiness, too. In reality, however, true Happiness is an *acquired character trait*, since it is actually an *inner* product acquired by developing one's personality and is *independent* of external events. Once one has achieved happiness, he can truly keep it forever.

We find this exciting idea in the writings of the Saba of Kelm (*Chachmah U'Mussar* II, p. 331): "As Aristotle has written, 'property belongs to a person externally. Character traits, however, belong to one intrinsically.' [Aristotle] devotes a whole chapter to the question: How should one be happy if one is not wealthy, considering that happiness depends on wealth? He answers, that a happy person would not forgo his happiness, no matter what the obstacle."

Rav Shimshon Raphael Hirsch writes (on *Bamidbar* 10:10): "Happiness is not necessarily the elevated feeling that comes from a particular cause. Rather, it includes the feelings of gladness of heart and the soul's own internal joy which ought to fill us *all the time*. This is indicated in the verses (Psalms 90): 'We are satisfied by Your kindness in the morning, and we rejoice and are glad all our lives'...."

As we know from the study of *Mussar* (the Jewish ethical teachings), desired virtues *can* be developed until they become secondnature. Thus, once one has internalized happiness, he or she can actually be happy and even joyous all the time!

Rav Dessler makes the point that "When [the month of] *Adar* begins, one increases joyfulness" (*Ta'anit* 29a) — How? By *developing* it in himself, so that one's happiness actually increases from day to day.

Since happiness is acquired by working on one's character, rather than by depending on outside circumstances, every one of us can reach and achieve happiness, for we only need to actively implant and cultivate it in our hearts.

The Steps to Happiness

The way that one acquires this worthwhile character trait is, *one step at a time*. There are many specific positive mental attitudes which contribute to the all-encompassing virtue of happiness, and they are all acquired by the same two steps. First, one must develop a true understanding of the particular attitude and the subject to which it relates, and second, one must then take this profound *da'at* (understanding) and use it to control one's instinctive feelings. When one's feelings are governed by reason, even the deepest sorrow can be overcome.

2

OBSERVING CREATION

Insight

The key to opening the Gate of Happiness is the attribute we call "understanding" (*da'at* or *de'ah*).

The *Gemara* records (*Nedarim* 41a):

> "Abbaye said, 'In our opinion, the poor person is one who lacks understanding.' In Eretz Yisrael they said, 'One who has understanding has everything, while one who does not have understanding has nothing.'"

Rashi explains that, one who has *da'at* has everything and lacks nothing, [for one who lacks a true understanding of life, all the property he owns counts as nothing].

By "understanding" (*de'ah*), the *Gemara* means the intellect's ability to recognize the true value of things. As it says in the Talmud Yerushalmi (*Berachot* 5:2): "If there is no *de'ah*, how can one differentiate?" The faculty of the mind called "understanding" enables us to distinguish between things, as well as to weigh and determine their relative importance. One who has developed this faculty can be truly happy, because he can appreciate whatever he has, starting with the miraculous gift of life itself. One who does not have this understanding will not be happy with all the wealth in the world, since he will not know how to appreciate it properly. Until you have developed this understanding, acquiring new possessions will *never* make you happy. Once you acquire the ability to appreciate what you have, you realize that acquiring new possessions is no longer necessary. "If you have acquired Understanding, what else are you missing?" (*Nedarim* ibid.)

Lack of understanding can be exemplified by a child's appreciation of a jewel. The "shiny rock," cannot make the child happy because he is unable to recognize its true worth. Similarly, when a child complains jealously over the differences between the sweets which he and a friend have been given, he is suffering from an inability to recognize actual worth. He should be happy with what he has.

Often, we too, lack understanding. We feel resentful about trivialities which we are missing, while ignoring the significance of that which we already have. We will arrive at a state of happiness when we become more aware of the great amount of good HaShem does for all of us every day of our lives.

Blessed Be He Who Created All These to Serve Me

Far more than previous generations, our generation has been blessed with a bounty of blessings and innovations for our benefit and comfort. Yet most of these blessings go unnoticed and are taken for granted. The way to overcome this lack of awareness is by kindling the light of the heart, which in turn enlightens the eyes to observe and become aware. The attitude which results from an appreciation of the abundance of lovingkindness bestowed upon us is the fundamental basis for achieving contentment within our lives. A person whose eyes are open emerges from his world of sleepy discontent into a new, wonderful world, full of light and gratitude.

We learn in *Sefer Be'er Avraham* (commentary on *Tehillim* — Psalms 33):

> "If we observe the many things that the Merciful Father has created for His children, for their benefit and joy, the skies will smile and shine upon us with their celestial hosts that are 'full of glow and radiate brightness.' By His Will, the sun and the moon give us illumination; the land is full of a variety of delicious fruits and vegetation; the animals are at our service for nutriment and work; the birds sing in the skies to please us, enhance our spirits and imbue our hearts with joy; the waters of the rivers, the oceans and the depths provide us with varieties of fish in a multitude of species; and there are innumerable additional necessities essential for the life of man. HaShem, He is G-d Who dresses us with decorative garments; He prepares spacious and comfortable houses for us to dwell in. He has commanded all the creatures to serve us, as a king commands all to serve his beloved son. This observation is recommended and positive [for the sake of man and] in His honor, as HaShem proclaims: 'Even every one that is called in My Name; for I have created him for My glory; I have formed him; indeed I have made him.'"

The person who is aware discovers the brightness and beauty that fills the world. He observes and grasps the significance of all its creatures and realizes that they are all in his service, just as servants to their master. He joyfully acknowledges the kindness of the Creator and is full of gratitude towards Him.

All that Exists — for the Sake of Man

Our "spiritual nearsightedness" is an obstacle which once overcome, will enable us to observe the endless abundance of benefits which are freely and continually being heaped upon us.

For the entire world is a gift from the Creator to all mankind.

In the Talmud we find (*Shabbat* 77b):

> "Rav Yehuda said, 'Whatever the Holy One, Blessed be He, created in His world, He created nothing in vain.' "

The Rambam (in his introduction to *Z'raim*) elaborates on this Talmudic principle in the following enlightening words:

> "In general, it should be known that all that exists under the circle of the moon exists for the sake of man alone. Of the various animals, some are for man's food, such as cattle and sheep; some are for other needs, such as the donkey which carries what is too heavy for man, and the horse which travels long distances in a short time. There are some spe-

cies whose benefits to man are difficult to discern, but man does benefit from them, even though he may not be aware of it.

The same applies to the trees and vegetation. Some are for man's sustenance and others for healing him from disease.

Anything that is found among the animals and the vegetables that is not edible and according to our understanding is of no benefit, is due to our limited wisdom. There simply cannot be any grass or fruit, nor any species of animal, from the elephant to the worm, which is of no benefit to man. In every generation we discover new value in previously unappreciated species. Man's mind is incapable of understanding the benefit of each and every animal and vegetation on the earth, but he can comprehend that [these benefits exist], judging from the experiences of past generations."

Examples

There is nothing without its purpose for mankind. We shall point to two examples to illustrate the words of the Rambam: "In every generation we discover new value in previously unappreciated species":

One example — oil (petrol) was deposited in the depths of the earth for thousands of years, an inaccessible and useless substance. Today, this "black gold" meets the most vital technological needs of modern society, by producing diskettes, heating our homes and fueling our cars.

Another example — a green blade of grass absorbs carbon dioxide from the air we breath. A rabbit eats the grass. A vulture preys on the rabbit. The vulture dies and the microbes disintegrate the corpse, and so, the gas returns to the air. All these creatures are necessary for the completion of the carbon dioxide cycle which is essential for the continuation of the world's ecosystem in which we live.

The Midrash says (*Bereshit Rabbah* 10:7): "Our Sages said, 'Even things that you consider unnecessary in the world, such as flies, fleas and mosquitos, are also essential to Creation, and everything has the destiny which the Creator designated for it, even the serpent, mosquito and frog.' "

A person who believes in HaShem knows that everything in this world was created with wisdom, and that it was created for the sake of man.

This World Was Created for Me

The mere recognition that everything was created for mankind is not enough. Each of us should be aware that the entire cosmos was created for him *personally*, that it was given to *him* as a gift from the Sovereign of the universe. As we learn in the words of our Sages (*Sanhedrin* 37a): "Every person is obligated to say 'For me this world was created.' "

Ben Zoma saw a very large crowd of people while standing on the stairs of the Temple Mount. He said (*Berachot* 58a):

> "Blessed is He, Who created all these to serve me... How much did Adam labor until he obtained bread to eat [in the Garden of Eden]? He plowed, seeded, harvested, threshed, sifted, grinded, kneaded and baked — and only then did he eat. But I wake up in the morning and find everything prepared for

me! How much did Adam have to toil until he had a garment to wear? He sheared, bleached, combed, spun and wove — and only then did he have a garment to wear. But I wake up in the morning and find all these prepared for me!... A good guest, what does he say? 'How much the host troubled himself for me, how much meat he brought before me, how much wine he served me; how many rolls he brought me — and all that trouble was for me!' But a bad guest, what does he say? 'For what purpose did this host trouble himself? I only ate one piece of bread, I had just one piece of meat, I only drank one glass — all the host's trouble was just for his own wife and children!' "

We shall begin to explain the words of this Talmudic passage from its end: A good guest who is invited for dinner by his friend and finds a set table, with bread sliced and portions prepared on beautiful platters, thinks in his heart of all the trouble the host went through for him. A bad guest, on the other hand, thinks that the host went through the trouble solely for his own sake and for the sake of his family, and that the effort for him was negligible.

Thus, this passage explains the benediction that Ben Zoma recited. When he observed a gathering of people, Ben Zoma recognized all sorts of craftsmen: a farmer, a baker, a cook, etc. He knew that every person did his job faithfully, such as the baker, who produced a large quantity of bread for the entire city each day. Yet although only one of these loaves actually reached Ben Zoma, his blessing wisely reflected the appreciative attitude that all "the host" did was for him alone.

Every individual should behave as a good guest in the world of the Holy One, Blessed be He. He should think that the Host created and made everything just for him, even though innumerable others also enjoy the Creator's works. The Talmud ends with: "About the good guest, what does [the host] say? 'Remember that you magnify His work which men behold.' " This is to say that the good guest is ultimately praising and exalting the works of HaShem, Who created everything in His world to serve man.

Looking Deeper to Appreciate More Fully

Every single act of creation constitutes a special, personal gift which should inspire us to feel indebted. We should learn to ponder, appreciate and rejoice over each element of our daily lives, and then to give thanks.

For this reason, Rabbi Yehuda would give thanks for the rain with the following words: "We must give thousands upon thousands of blessings and thanksgiving unto Your Name for every single drop that You bring down for us." In another passage, our Sages say (*Midrash Rabbah, Bereshit* 14:9): "Rabbi Levi said in the name of Rabbi Chanina, 'For every single breath that one breathes, he should praise the Holy One, blessed be He, in the words of the Biblical verse: Let every soul that has breath praise HaShem. Praise You, HaShem.' "

In the Book of Ruth (2:2) we see how Ruth gathered sheaves of barley for her mother-in-law, Naomi. Although Ruth's harvest included chaff and straw in addition to the edible grains, she made certain to bring only the grains to her mother-in-law (2:17): "She gleaned in the field until evening, beat out that which she had gleaned, and it amounted to just about an *ephah* of barley."

Naomi was not satisfied with simply thanking Ruth for the *ephah* of barley which she received. She verbally made the effort to *observe* and *appreciate* the trouble Ruth had gone through — actually gathering much more than an *ephah* of barley. Therefore, it says (2:18): "And her mother-in-law saw what she had gathered [rather than seeing only what Ruth gave her]" (according to the commentary of the Gra). Naomi realized that she was obliged to inquire about the kindness of their benefactor, and therefore, she not only gave thanks for what she received, but inquired further in order to fully appreciate even what was not apparent.

Let's follow Naomi's example, to consider the almost endless chain of kindness necessary for the production of even the simplest of our needs.

Practical Observations

"Blessed be the Name of the King of Kings, the Holy One, Blessed be He, Who created His world with wisdom and understanding, there are no equals to His wonders and there is no count to His greatness" (*Midrash Rabbah*, *Bamidbar* 18:22).

If we study this midrash further, we see that the wondrous deeds of the Creator are enumerated in great detail. The *Eliyahu Rabbah* (Chapter 2) also describes at length the wonders of creation. Similarly, the Rambam follows our Sages' example and devotes several chapters (2, 3 and 4 of *Hilchot Yesodei HaTorah*) to describing the route and the patterns of the stars and the planets, so that through this, a person may recognize the Divine wisdom, in order to awaken a love for HaShem within himself.

In every generation, more and more of the wonders of the Creator are revealed to us each day. We must follow in the footsteps of our sacred Rabbis and *apply* the knowledge that the Holy One, Blessed be He, has granted us, in order to understand the good that is given to us, and to become happy through it.

It is worthwhile to consider recent scientific discoveries of our own generation in order to fulfill our duty of observing the marvelous creations of HaShem.

Researchers now realize that even the smallest elements in nature, even those which seem very simple at a superficial glance, are actually infinitely involved, intricate and complicated in the most wondrous fashion. To understand this thoroughly one would have to spend many years in study. Our purpose here is to point out several examples amidst nature's infinite multitudes, so that our hearts will be awakened in awe and, we become happy with our lot.

Our Meal

Bread Sustains the Heart of Man

When you chew on a slice of bread, do you take the time and effort to realize how much there is in that slice to become elated about? If we would only consider the great gift that a slice of bread in our hand represents, we would certainly appreciate the wondrous processes involved. Let's look more closely now into the many and varied aspects that go into the growth, production and utilization of our bread.

The Leaf

Every plant and vegetable product — including, of course, the wheat grain, source of our bread — is created in a "laboratory" with which even the most advanced and sophisticated man-made laboratories cannot compare. Each leaf is covered with epidermises, transparent cells which are specially designed to allow the sun's rays to penetrate them, while at the same time, preventing the leaf from drying out. In-between these cells, there are other cells which create tiny holes that enable air to filter through the leaf.

Further investigation reveals that the top outer layer of the leaf is comprised of structures known as chloroplasts, with millions in every leaf. In itself, the chloroplast is a complicated structure, containing all the chemical materials necessary for producing the nutrients needed by each leaf. It also includes scores of "granaries," in which this process of nutrient formation takes place. Every granary constitutes a formation of a great variety of molecules arranged in a very unusual pattern. Even more, each molecule is made up of particles and parts of particles that are, in themselves, comprised of atoms revolving around each other at a tremendous velocity in precise formation. And all of this stunning coordination is absolutely essential for the functioning of each and every leaf!

Thus, we find that even something as seemingly insignificant as the outer structure of a leaf can evoke reverence and awe in our hearts towards the Master of Wisdom, Who has engineered this miraculous creation.

Let us stop for a moment to ponder and appreciate the vast micro-world of the leaf. In order to better grasp the magnitude of each leaf's complexity, imagine that every molecule in the leaf is a person, and that all of these people are joined together to form a gigantic army of *millions* of battalions, each battalion comprised of a large number of soldiers. Every soldier is posted in a particular location and is in charge of a specific task. All the battalions and individual soldiers are essential for the efficient functioning of the entire army. Together, simultaneously, the multitudes of the soldiers join together in executing the duties of the battalion, and all the battalions join together to achieve the army's goal. This is what takes place in the small leaf as it continually deploys its tremendous "army" for the production of its nutrition.

The number of ingredients in the leaf-laboratory is so enormous, that if every molecule in a leaf was the size of a test tube, no continent would be large enough to contain them all. Furthermore, the chemical processes in the leaf are so complex, that science, despite intensive study and observation, has not yet approached a complete understanding of them.

The Elemental Building Blocks

Let's look a bit further into the amazing nutrient factory which is in every plant. The plant's roots work like a quarry, boring deep into the ground and drawing up water and various dissolved minerals. The chemical process in the leaf creates energy which works like a powerful pump to lift the water and minerals from the ground up to the leaf despite gravity. No matter how tall the tree, water and minerals always manage to rise from the ground to the leaves at its top.

The sun, which is actually a huge natural atomic reactor, provides the energy for the leaf to execute the chemical processes necessary for generating the nutriments. Once the various materials have reached the leaves, another chemical process unites the water with the oxygen in the air, creating sugar. The complex process continues, and the sugar turns into starches, creating vitamins vital for human existence. This "manufactured product" then continues through "pipes" that bring it all up to build the fruits, vegetables, grains, wood and fibers we need, all in accordance with the Creator's Master Plan.

How wondrous is the fact that the tiny leaf creates human nourishment from the dead earth and from the lifeless air !

The Rain

Let us not forget the rain that provides water for the growth of the wheat plant. The miraculous water cycle: The sun acts as a mighty pump and raises great volumes of water from the seas; the air vapor is concentrated in the form of clouds; the clouds hold billions of gallons of vaporized water and somehow manage to retain their precious treasure until HaShem's air transporter, the wind, blows them to their destinations. There, specialized unloaders, cold air currents, transform the vapor back into drops of water — rain. Then HaShem's cargo worker, gravity, transports the water to its final destination where it brings life to all plant and animal life. Surplus water is eventually transported back to the sea where it is ready to repeat the cycle again and again.

Furthermore, since there are not always "flights arriving" from far-off seas, so that plants can survive the intervals between the water supplies, HaShem sends dew on a daily basis to supply them with life-giving moisture. The Talmud (*Ta'anit* 3a) says that the dew and the winds never stop. Rashi explains that, were it not so, the world could not exist.

All man-made transport techniques are but dim shadows compared to the magnificent rain cycle, devised and created with Divine wisdom and miraculous precision, about which the verse says (Job 5:8): "...Who does great and unsearchable things; marvelous things without number; Who gives rain upon the earth, and sends waters upon the fields."

The Crafts

We should also bear in mind the sophisticated machinery that is necessary to plow, seed and harvest the crops and to separate the wheat grains from the chaff; to grind the flour and store it in huge magazines. The trucks and transporters that bring the wheat to the factory and the bread to the houses involve sophisticated technology as well. These man-made innovations were all developed from the basic materials of Creation, and it is the Creator Who grants man the intelligence and wisdom necessary to assemble and benefit from these materials.

The Digestive Process

Granted that the mineral-to-bread production process is wondrous, but the process through which we consume and digest our food is more amazing still. Our tongue pushes the food from side to side in our mouth so that the teeth can grind it. Glands secrete saliva which dilutes the food and begins the digestive process.

Simultaneously, the stomach begins producing acids designed to consume every type of food while not affecting the flesh of the stomach itself, even though it is comprised of the very same materials as the food!

Our liver produces gall that drips into the intestines in just the right quantity necessary for each particular kind of food. From the intestines thousands upon thousands of pipes distribute the digested food to all parts of the body, supplying every limb and organ with the exact quantity it requires.

In order to digest various foods, hundreds of chemical factors turn poisonous materials in the body into useful materials. Every chemical has its name and task: nicotinamide, benzoic acid, alcohols, aromatic acids and more. For example, excess nitrogen turns into urea through ATP and other organic catalysts.

Besides the chemical processes these chemicals induce, they are also capable of processing the poisonous material in remarkably short periods of time and at surprisingly low temperatures. Scientists have found that for certain foods which the human body successfully digests in only four hours, it would be necessary to cook the same food for 24 hours, in boiling water *along* with a very strong acid, in order to dissolve it outside the body!

Bread: In Conclusion

We find, therefore, that innumerable elements and processes are necessary for providing "simple" bread for man, from the threshing of the wheat until its final digestion in the body. The tiny grain of wheat is the result of the labor of billions of molecules and chemical materials that are all messengers of the Creator in the service of providing us with nourishment. "How vast are Your deeds, HaShem, You have created all with wisdom, the universe is full of Your accomplishments" (Psalms 104:24).

Livelihood

There is also something miraculous about making one's living and being able to procure a loaf of bread. Our Sages have already remarked (*Pesachim* 118a): "Providing a person's livelihood is as difficult as the division of the Red Sea, as we read: 'He provides bread for all flesh' (Psalms 136:25) and just before it, 'He Who divided the Red Sea into portions. (ibid., 136:12)' " The Rashbam (ibid.) explains: "This is to say that the Holy One, Blessed be He, performs just as great a miracle for the person for whom He provides sustenance as He did for the Israelites when He split the Red Sea."

Additional Observations: The Rest of the Meal

All of what we have discussed is but a mere drop in the ocean of the abundance of benefits continually being conferred upon us. For "Man does not live by bread alone." There are other types of nourishment in every meal, each with an array of miraculous processes of its own.

For example: HaShem created various delicious and nutritious foods. The pleasurable good taste of each one actually *encourages* us to nourish ourselves! Moreover, the great variety of tantalizing tastes and aromas actually represent each of the food groups necessary for a person's health. A well-planned meal with regard to taste is also a perfectly balanced meal from the standpoint of nutrition.

Thus, although bread satisfies one's hunger, it lacks any special taste. Therefore, HaShem has designed the world so that after breaking bread, a person still desires additional foods to complete his meal. There are the pickled foods that are appetizing and stimulate one to eat more. Afterwards, vegetables, meat and eggs are added to the meal, complementing the bread to give it taste. When a person has had enough to eat, a sweet fruit for dessert limits the appetite and completes the meal. In this way, we receive all the food groups that are necessary for our nourishment: starches from the bread, proteins from the meat, milk or fish, plus minerals and sugars from the fruits, etc.

The Completion of Digestion

HaShem has created the plants we eat in such a manner that they contain various materials which ease the human digestive process. For example, in order to digest sugars and carbohydrates, an abundance of Vitamin B is necessary. Raw sugar contains an abundance of Vitamin B! In other words, the "smart" plant selects from the ground precisely those vitamins which we require to complete its digestive process in our bodies.

Another example: In order to absorb Vitamin C, Vitamin P is necessary. The inner, white part of any citrus fruit's peel actually constitutes a rich source of Vitamin P, which then helps the body to absorb the Vitamin C contained in the citrus fruit itself !

Brought from Far Away

In the *Gemara* we discussed earlier (*Berachot* 58a) Ben Zoma says: "All nationalities come to the door of my house, and I rise in the morning and find all these before me." The Maharsha explains: "Obviously all nations need one another, for what one lacks can be found in the other. The merchants bring from the place of supply to the place of demand. Ben Zoma was appreciative and thankful to the Creator of the world for providing him with the people who serve him by bringing him his necessities from far away places."

The transport of food over great distances has been advanced and developed tremendously in our age. Every country in the world possesses different natural resources. Thanks to modern means of shipping and transporting, everyone in the world has the opportunity to enjoy all the good things that G-d has granted mankind. Huge freight ships and gigantic aircraft transport commodities from all corners of the earth: meat from Argentina, fish from Norway, rice from Japan, wheat from the United States, pineapple from Africa. Furthermore, not everyone is aware of all the chemical materials which were artificially introduced into his meal, materials which were themselves manufactured in all parts of the world. It is difficult to imagine the vast numbers of people who are employed in perfecting our food. Furthermore, how many people does it take to construct the food factories, or to build the ships and the trucks and to run them! Once again, taking time to observe awakens our awareness, which fans the flames of our appreciation and awe. "Blessed is He Who created all these to serve me !"

Blessings

In order to induce us to take the time to observe, our Sages constructed an elegant collection of *berachot* encompassing the entire Creation and the various benefits HaShem provides us through that Creation. There are *berachot* over the various foods we eat to maintain our lives. Each type of food is unique, and our Sages instituted a special *berachah* for each type of food in order that we take note of its uniqueness (bread, fruits, vegetables, etc.). There is a *berachah* for the pleasure we derive from the various plants and flowers that fill the world with their fragrance. There are *berachot* over the wonderous forces of nature: the illuminating lightning and the roaring thunder, the high seas, the vast oceans and the great rivers, the tall mountains and the marvelous canyons. Upon beholding one of these phenomena, we recite: "Blessed be HaShem, Creator of the Wonders of Creation."

All these *berachot* were devised with the purpose of uplifting our souls to grasp the wonders of Creation. The *Kuzari* writes (*Maamar* 3:15):

> "Surely the mature person experiences pleasure far more than a baby or an animal. Similarly, if a drunkard were to be given all possible pleasure while he was drunk, when he sobers up and realizes what he has essentially forfeited, he would surely regret how much he has missed, because he had been numb to it all.
>
> This, then, is the benefit of the *berachot*. They are instrumental in helping us *to take notice* of life's many pleasures, *to be aware* of

them in our heart and soul. A person should
take to heart the meaning of each and every
blessing and understand its intention and significance. One who does not do so does not
enjoy life like a human being, but rather, like
an animal or a baby."

Through the *berachot* our Sages implemented new possibilities for perception and inspiration. Let's analyze two
berachot and attempt to understand their significance.

Brachah A —"All was Created by His Word"

Reb Yisroel Salanter Ztz"l (of blessed memory), once noticed that in an exclusive restaurant an unreasonable sum
of money was charged for a cup of tea. He approached the
proprietor and asked him why the cup of tea was so expensive. After all, a cup of hot water, a few tea leaves and a
spoonful of sugar could not amount to more than a couple
of pennies, he argued.

Smiling, the proprietor answered Reb Yisroel. "Indeed,
your figure is just about right, sir; however, for a couple of
pennies, please be honored to have tea in your own home.
Here in the restaurant, with the beautiful chandeliers, the
music in the background, the exquisite view, the waiters in
their colorful uniforms with golden buttons and the tea
that is served you in an artistically ornamented china cup
— all *this* costs money!"

Reb Yisroel's face lit up. "Oh, thank you, thank you so
very much!"

The owner was puzzled. "Why are you thanking me so
enthusiastically?" he inquired.

"My dear fellow," Reb Yisroel smiled, "due to your fascinating explanation, I now understand the benediction of "Shehakol — All Was Created by His Word" which we recite before we drink water. You see, until now, when I recited this blessing I had in mind only that I am thanking the Creator for the water that He created. Now, however, I understand the blessing much better. 'All' includes not merely the water but also the fresh air that we breathe while drinking the water, the beautiful world around us, the music of the birds that entertain us and exalt our spirits, each with its different voice, the charming flowers with their splendid colors and marvelous hues, the fresh breeze — for all *this* we have to thank HaShem when drinking our water!"

Similarly, in the *Bircat HaMazon* (Grace after Meal), we thank HaShem for a "desirable, good and broad land." HaGaon HaTzadik Rav Yechezkel Levinstein, Ztz"l, pointed out that we thank HaShem not merely for the food, but also for the beauty of the Land of Israel itself.

Berachah B — The Blossom of the Tree

When we see a blossoming tree that bears edible fruit, we recite: "Blessed...Whose world lacks nothing." Why was this blessing instituted upon the tree when it is blossoming? After all, other *Birchot HaNehenin* (Benedictions over Enjoyments) are to be said only upon partaking of the food or fragrance itself, not for its appearance.

The following analogy offers an explanation: Two people were invited to dine with the king. The first was an important official, who was served in exclusive utensils decorated with a beautiful floral pattern in accordance with his high status. The second was an ordinary person of low rank. Although the food he was served was the same as that served to the man of higher status, it was served on simple dishes. Similarly, the tree provides us with fruit in a gorgeous setting of leaves, buds and flowers. We therefore praise the King of Glory that not merely does He provide all His creatures with sustenance and nourishment, but He even gives us our livelihood with dignity, in "dishes" that are beautiful to the eye, adorned and ornamented with magnificent flowers so that, in rapture, we may testify: "Not a thing is lacking in His world!"

Thus, we have here a wonderful method to intensify our awareness. The *berachot* help us to perceive and appreciate within our hearts and minds all of the great benefits we constantly enjoy, to take note of them and through them to ascend to Simchah!

Conclusion

A person through careful observation will find that countless benefits surround him constantly. Each and every benefit is the product of a long sequence of miraculous events.

Unfortunately, the great light that shines from this endless array of good often blinds us from perceiving their true significance. Our minds are incapable of grasping so many awe-inspiring perceptions at one time. Let us train ourselves to be aware of the precious gifts given to us by the Creator. If we practice focusing our attention on *one item at a time*, we will gradually increase our ability to understand the magnitude of each benefit in depth.

True comprehension of even the smallest of these blessings can kindle the warm glow of contentment, thus filling the heart with happiness. Moreover, this practice will also help us maintain our interest and enthusiasm for the many blessings we enjoy. After we absorb one item, we can go on to the next. The process is endless, for the *chessed* (lovingkindness) of HaShem has no end....

3

AWARENESS THROUGH EXCITEMENT

We have just discussed the first step towards happiness, the observation and appreciation of all we have. However, intellectual observation is not sufficient to turn happiness into an internal trait. Another ingredient is required: excitement of the heart, as we shall explain further, with G-d's help.

The Tendency to Get Used to Things

In view of the abundance of benefits that miraculously surround us by the grace of HaShem, the puzzling question arises: Why are we not naturally aware of these benefits? Why do we tend to relate to them as insignificant and take them for granted?

The *Chovot HaLevavot* (Introduction to *Sha'ar HaBechinah*) explains this phenomenon in an analogy: A person was walking in the wilderness when he found an abandoned baby. He brought the child to his home, and fully provided for it, until the child grew up and became an adult. Later, the benevolent man heard about another person, someone who had fallen into captivity. He saved him, but actually did for him only a fraction of what he had done for the baby. However, the captive will be immeasurably more appreciative towards his benefactor than the child, even though the child received a great deal more than the captive. This is because all the favors and benefits which the child received from his adoptive father were constantly present throughout his life and had come to seem customary and *natural* to him.

It is the same with us, explains the *Chovot HaLevavot*. Since we are used to the miraculous beneficence of HaShem from our childhood, it becomes routine and normal in our eyes, as if it is an integral part of our very existence. Thus, we tend neither to appreciate the value of all this goodness, nor the One Who gives it to us.

The Talmud (*Berachot* 57b) greatly praises the value of the sun, to the extent of comparing its benefit with the World to Come. Reb Yisroel Salanter, Ztz"l, would always praise the sun. It is truly surprising that we ignore the greatness of its benefits. In contrast, when we go outdoors on a pitch black night and lightning suddenly explodes upon our surroundings, we are thrilled by the marvelous sight; and this impression will remain with us. How can we explain our excitement over the lightning which illuminates a small area of land for just a brief moment and from a nearby source, in comparison to our indifference concerning the sun, which is "full of light and radiates brightness" (*Shabbat* prayer) continuously, from a distance of some 100 million miles, and illuminates not only a small area but "magnificent is its light in the entire world (ibid.)?!"

The Secret of Enthusiasm

The answer is that we are so accustomed to the sun that, paradoxically, in spite of its greatness, we forget its profound impressiveness.

From what we have said, we may conclude that the quality which diminishes our enthusiasm is *familiarity*. Adjusting to and getting accustomed to things makes us underestimate them, and overlook even the greatest factors in our lives. It is noteworthy that in Hebrew, the source of the word שכיח — usual or routine — is שכח, to forget. The heart tends to forget something that is usual and routine. Something new, on the other hand, is well remembered, as our Sages put it: "One remembers a new insight." The newer or more novel the event, the more profound its impression upon us.

The question then arises: Why is this so? How does the regularity of something diminish the excitement it engenders in us? What is the force that makes us forget to see the miraculous in the everyday? To explain this phenomenon, we can consider the following: Black print on white paper will stand out vividly. The sharper the contrast between a written text and its background, the stronger the print's impression on the viewer. The same is true regarding impressions on one's mind and heart. The greater the contrast, the deeper the impression and the stronger the excitement.

If a person is granted a wonderful gift when he least expects it, he strongly feels the contrast between the existing moment and the previous moment when he lacked it, and he becomes very excited. Similarly, regarding the order of a meal: the custom is to start with a sweet or sharp appetizer, because such foods "open the heart to the meal" (*Mishnah Berurah* 176:2). The sharp contrast between not eating anything and then eating these things awakens the senses, and generates and amplifies a desire for the meal.

Sudden Joy

We learn in the Torah (*Bereshit* 45:26) how the sons of Ya'akov brought the good tidings that Yoseph was still alive: "And they told him *saying*, 'Yoseph is yet alive and he is the ruler over the entire land of Egypt.' " The *Or HaChaim* explains there: "The reason for the word 'saying' is that they told him the good news *wisely*, in a way that should not shock his heart. For it is well known that when good news comes when a person is grieving, and all the more so when the news is extremely good, it can be very dangerous and can shock him to the extent that he may suddenly die. Therefore, in their concern, they thought judiciously how to speak in a way that would not harm him. The verse says 'and they said to him, *saying*,' implying that they informed him that they had good news to tell him, so that his soul would open up and his heart become joyous. Only then did they say that Yosef was still alive, without endangering him, for his heart was prepared for receiving good news."

We see that when there is a strong emotional contrast, such as happy news about something wonderful which comes to a person while he is grieving, suddenly, without any previous preparation, it has a great impact on him to the extent that it can even be detrimental.

Indeed, we know of such events in history. The Talmud (*Ketubot* 62b) tells about such a death which resulted from sudden joy: Rav Hanania ben Chachinai went far from home to a place of Torah for thirteen years. He returned to his town and entered his home suddenly, unannounced, while his wife was busy with the housework. When she raised her head and saw him suddenly, her heart stopped beating and she died. Rashi adds that she had suddenly comprehended in her heart that it was her husband, and therefore, she died. Explains HaGaon Reb Chaim Shmulevitz, Ztz"l (*Sichot Mussar*, Yr. 5733, 6), that her heart had realized that it was her husband, before she had observed him well with her eyes. Had she noticed him previously, there would have been a slight pause between what her eyes saw and the feeling of her heart, and that would have eased her longing for her husband for whom she had been waiting many years. Then her joyous heart would have been able to withstand the shock. But now, when her heart comprehended before her eyes observed, her feelings overwhelmed her and her heart could not stand the immense joy at the sudden meeting.

The Secret of Familiarity

Since we have clarified the secret of enthusiasm, we can now understand the psychology of adaptation and familiarity. Just as the sharpness of the contrast intensifies the sense of excitement, so does the force of familiarity minimize enthusiasm. Familiarity diminishes the contrast, until one does not feel the value of what is given to him. Reb Chaim Shmulevitz explains (ibid.), that little by little, a man has the power to get used to even the most difficult things. "We have seen it in our own generation, when our brethren were trapped in the Nazi valley of death and unbearable torture was their daily lot. Our hair rises from hearing these stories. It is beyond our comprehension to understand how some of the people survived all of the devilish torment, when they were forcefully taken from their peaceful homes and cast into the swamp of blood-thirsty, two-legged beasts. How did they survive? The answer is that the transfer from the home to the inferno was gradual, and they *had gotten used to* one phase before going on to another, and so on, until they hit rock bottom. This is how some people managed to go through the seven spheres of *Gehennom*."

So, we see that this psychological mechanism, like all elements HaShem has instilled in His Creation, has its place. However, what about *overcoming* this tendency, instead of letting it blind us?

The Virtue of Enthusiasm

In order to overcome the tendency of getting used to things, which decreases our attention and awareness, the *Ba'alei Mussar* have instituted "Serving [of HaShem] through *Observation and Excitement*". Through this spiritual exercise, a person can *train* himself to sense the novelty in things and to actually become excited about it. Through this, he will learn to always feel joy for the limitless gifts in life.

The Sabah of Kelm asks in *Chachmah U'Mussar* (Vol. II, p. 219):

"*Klal Yisroel* reached the level of prophecy when they saw the wondrous signs and miracles in Egypt. Why, then, do we not reach the level of prophecy as well, since we believe through the tradition handed down by our ancestors that HaShem indeed performed the miracles for Israel?

What is the difference between seeing and intellectual knowledge [of the sight]?" The Sabah answers, that since we are so *accustomed* to things, habit makes us forget the excitement. For this reason, we do not reach the level to merit prophecy.

The Sabah revealed to us an awesome thought: that the difference between today's generation and the Congregation of Israel who saw vividly the revelation of His Kingdom is merely in the level of enthusiasm. If we could only contemplate the miracles that occurred to our forefathers in Egypt until we reached a certain level of enthusiasm and excitement, we too could attain their level of prophecy!

Acclimation to Miracles

According to this principle, we can now explain the Talmud (*Shabbat* 13b) that asks: Why do we not celebrate *Yom Tov* on all those days upon which HaShem performed miracles and wonders and delivered us from all our enemies? The *Gemara* answers: "Said Rabban Shimon ben Gamliel, 'We, too, are fond of the troubles. [We, too, are fond of the miracles which delivered us from the troubles, and would have loved to turn those days into *Yomim Tovim* — Rashi.] But what can we do? If we come to write them, there are too many [of these days].' "

Still, the question arises: So what if there are too many special days to observe them all, why not commemorate at least some of them? The answer is that we would be so accustomed to miracles and wonders that we would not get excited over *any* of the days of salvation, and therefore there is no sense in proclaiming them days of joy.

According to *Halachah*, we do not recite the blessing over fire except on *Motzei Shabbat* and *Motzei Yom Kippur*. The

Shitah Mekubetzet (*Berachot* 53b) explains the reason for this: "Actually, one should say a blessing over fire every night. However, since fire is used continuously, it would not be proper to recite the blessing. On *Motzei Shabbat* and *Motzei Yom Kippur*, however, when we have not used fire during the day, it is proper to say the blessing and praise HaShem." From this explanation, we learn that there is no blessing on something which we enjoy continuously, only on the renewal of an interrupted or new pleasure.

Tapping the Moment

There is a very effective method, through the blessings, to avoid the pitfall of habit and routine: We can and must awaken ourselves to the potential excitement available at the very moment of greatest contrast — precisely when something *happens*.

A New Day

When Adam was created by the Holy One, Blessed be He, he saw before his eyes a new and marvelous world. How intense was his excitement at that time; how deep was his appreciation of his Maker, how enthusiastically he sang, "A Psalm, a song for the day of Shabbat: It is good to give thanks to HaShem and to sing to Your Name, oh Exalted One!" (According to the Midrash, Adam recited this psalm when he was created.)

This feeling could and *should* envelop every Jew when he wakes up each morning. The Rashba (quoted in *Mishnah Berurah*, *Orach Chaim* 4:1) writes: "This is because at dawn, after sleep, we become a new creation, in the words of the verse: 'New every morning, great is Your faithfulness.' Therefore, we are obligated to thank Him, to serve Him and to bless His holy Name. It is for this reason that all the morning *berachot* were instituted."

In order to not forget all the benefits that are being conferred upon us constantly, our Sages instituted the *Birchot HaShachar*. After a night's sleep, during which a person is powerless, he wakes up in the morning rejuvenated, his "batteries recharged." He should appreciate his renewed state, and for that reason we say: "המחזיר נשמות לפגרים מתים" — "He Who returns souls to dead corpses." In addition, one has to thank HaShem for all the individual capacities that were given him: the ability to walk, "המכין מצעדי גבר" — "He Who prepares the steps of man", and for the ability of balancing his body, "זוקף כפופים" — "He Who makes the stooped stand upright."

Similarly, when he opens his eyes in the morning, a person should remember that he has come from a world of darkness into a world full of light. He can now look into the holy letters of the Torah, he can enjoy the marvelous view, observe the sparkle of the sun on the waves, and the glitter in a child's eyes. With tremendous joy, he should bless "פוקח עוורים" — "He Who opens the eyes of the blind." Every limb in our body is comprised of countless particles that are assembled with the most wondrous coordination, with Divine wisdom, beyond our comprehension. Every morning we must literally and figuratively awaken ourselves to the feeling that the Holy One, Blessed be He, creates and renews every single cell of the many tens of thousands of the veins, muscles, fibres and tissues in our body.

Says the Sabah of Slobodka (*Ohr Tzafun* p. 100): When a

person gets up in the morning and finds a place to put his feet on the ground, and the sky stretches above him, he should feel that Hashem, at this very moment, has separated the water and the earth — creating the sky over his head and laying down the dry land under his feet. That in every step that he takes, HaShem has just then prepared that place for him to walk upon: "רוקע הארץ על המים" — "He Who spreads the land above the water."

Creator of the Lights

At the moment of dawn, when the sun's first rays break through, the sun "goes forth in all its might," and the day begins. At this moment, we must say the blessing:

"ברוך אתה ה' יוצר המאורות"
— Blessed are You, HaShem, Creator of the Lights."

It is explained in the Talmud (*Berachot* 9b):

> "Rav Yochanan said, *Vatikin* [Hebrew for veterans or seniors, the Sages of old] conclude it at *sunrise*.... Rav Zeyra said, What is the verse [upon which this is based]? 'They shall revere You *as the sun endures*, those who seek Your Face.' "

Rashi comments (ibid.): "This is to say that the moment the sun rises, *then* they revere You". Rashi comments further (*Berachot* 29b) that the Talmud is referring to the blessing "יוצר המאורות," — that one is actually commanded to recite it at sunrise.

The reason is that it is specifically at that moment when the sun rises, that a person is capable of becoming enthralled by the wondrous sight of the sun. (Actually, the blessing can be recited during the first quarter of the day, because the sun is still considered in its renewal-phase, and one can still become excited when witnessing the great luminary.) Thus, we see how the Sages have taken into consideration and utilized our tendency to be excited by contrast, as we discussed above.

New Life

Winter has passed. The trees that were standing like dead corpses are blooming again; life is renewed. At that moment of the renewal of the fruit cycle, a Jew is obligated to recite:

"ברוך. . .שלא חיסר בעולמו דבר ובא בו בריות טובות
ואילנות טובים ליהנות ליהנות בהם בני אדם"

— "Blessed...Whose world is not deficient in anything, and Who created in it good creatures and good trees for the pleasure of man."

Later, when the tree yields its goodness, producing new fruit, we recite: "ברוך...שהחיינו וקיימנו והגיענו לזמן הזה" — "Blessed...Who kept us alive and sustained us, and made us reach this time." Precisely at the "take-off" of the season of renewal, a person is actually capable of becoming elated over the fruit: the sweetness of its taste, its intriguing aroma, the spectrum and harmony of its colors and shades. As we learn in the Torah (Bereshit 2:9): "HaShem made every tree that is pleasant to the sight and good for food, grow out of the ground."

On the Day of the Rejoicing of His Heart

Our Sages also enacted a special *obligation* to rejoice on the day of one's wedding, again tapping the energy and enthusiasm generated by the new at its inception. Similarly, on the day that the cornerstone is laid for the erection of the Jewish home, the groom and bride should experience a sense of joy and happiness which will serve as a foundation and model for their life together.

Conclusion

We have seen that the way for us to feel a sense of renewal is to consciously appreciate the enumerable gifts HaShem bestows precisely at the very *moment* they begin. Our Sages instituted:

— That we bless HaShem for creating us anew every day just as we awaken each morning (*Birchat HaShachar*).

— That we bless HaShem for the renewal of the great luminary as each night opens into another day (*Yotzer HaMe'orot*).

— That we bless HaShem for agricultural abundance at the offset of each fruit's season ("Whose world is not deficient of anything" and *Shehecheyanu*).

— That we rejoice over the initiation of the construction of the Jewish home on the day of a wedding.

Just as produce will not thrive unless the seeds are sown in the appropriate season, so, it is difficult for the human heart to become enthralled and awed unless we grasp the opportunity to consider the wonders of the Creator at the *very moment* of their renewal.

The Concept of "What Is" as Opposed to "What Isn't"

We learn in *Novi Michah* (7:8): "Do not rejoice against me, my enemy. When I fall, I shall arise; when I sit in darkness, HaShem [will be] a light for me." Our Sages commented in the Midrash (*Shocher Tov, Tehillim* 2): "Had I not fallen, I would not stand up; had I not sat in the darkness, HaShem would not be a light for me." Here, a psychological secret is revealed to us: The good is alluring only in the face of the *lack* of it. When a person desires something and feels that he is lacking it, his desire for it intensifies in his heart. Then, when the deficiency is filled, he will fully appreciate the good.

The Enthusiasm of the Chachmei HaMussar

The *Gedolei HaMussar*, the Masters of Ethical Behavior, often emphasized their rapture over the good, particularly when its presence was highlighted in the face of the deficient.

The Sabah of Kelm was once on a long journey together with a group of escorts. When they ran out of food and drink, they noticed a small house in the distance. Knocking on the door, they politely requested some food, but the "generous" man gave them nothing more than some bread and water. Writes the Sabah (*Chachmah U'Mussar* ll, p. 74): "That meager portion of bread which sufficed for only one meal tasted so delicious, that I felt such joy and satisfaction eating it, more than when I eat a plethora of delicacies at home!"

Reb Yerucham of Mir, Ztz"l, relates (*Da'at Chachmah U'Mussar* III, p. 34) that one morning the weather was so bad that he was very sorry he had not taken his gloves. When someone was then kind enough to lend him a pair, he then realized their great value.

Another example of how not having leads one to appreciate what he does have: A prominent Torah scholar was very ill and bedridden for a long time. He relates that HaGaon Reb Mordechai Gifter, Shlita (Head of the Telz Yeshiva), would visit him, highly praising his own Rebbe, HaGaon Reb Eliyahu Meir Bloch, Ztz"l, for his great devotion to learning Torah. Even when Reb Bloch was ill and weak, he did not give up his regular learning sessions in the Yeshiva. When he was suffering pain to the extent that he was unable to learn a Talmudic discourse, he would study the less demanding Five Books of the Torah with its classic commentary by Rashi, even when that study, too, often had to be interrupted due to his condition. At the time, the previously sick scholar notes, he did not realize the great mental forces which were necessary for learning Torah with Rashi, until he himself experienced such weakness that he was unable to concentrate on learning anything. Now that he has recuperated, he appreciates even the ability to move a finger, and he can recite with tremendous joy: "ברוך הנותן ליעף כח" — "Blessed is He Who gives strength to the weary."

To Contemplate "Not Having" Just When You Have

Even when a particular pleasure is easily obtained, we

must consider how we would feel had we *lacked* it. Otherwise, we take for granted the advantages that seem to us matter-of-fact.

The *Kuzari* writes (Third *Ma'amar*, 17):

> "When you recite the blessing *Shehecheyanu V'kiyemanu* (in which one thanks G-d for having lived until that particular good moment), you should have in mind that you *could* have died, and thank HaShem for having kept you alive. Consider your life as something that you have been awarded... When the person thinks about its previous absence, *his enjoyment is manifold*."

In other words, when you thank HaShem for something that you enjoy, think what life would have been like had you *not* had it, and how you would have suffered without it. In this way, you will greatly amplify your sense of enjoyment.

The Sabah of Kelm expressed himself in the following words (*Chachmah U'Musar* II, p. 74): "The wise man — who imagines himself lacking what he has now — would surely be constantly in immense joy. Happy is his lot in this world and in the World to Come."

Practical Illustrations

The Water We Drink

In our age of technology and progress when we are the slightest bit thirsty, we need only to open the faucet to drink a glass of cool, clean water. Because the water is so simple for us to get, so routine, like breathing air, we become numbed to the blessing over the water, without which there is no life at all.

Instead, in order to stimulate the sense of elation over the lovingkindness of HaShem Who created water, the thinking man should imagine himself in a desert. The scorching sun is overhead, sweat is pouring down his face, his quest for a drop of water is so intense that he is about to lose his mind... yet there is no water in sight. Suddenly, the sound of running water is heard in the distance! With his last bit of energy, he runs, climbs mountains and descends valleys until he discovers the source of the water. Who can describe his ecstasy when he opens his mouth and drinks his fill of the precious, lifesaving fluid!

Why not consider this every time we have a drink of water, the elixir of life!

Technological Innovations

Technological progress fails to impress us today, since we are accustomed to it. The invention of the first airplane caused great excitement and joy in the world. Can you imagine! From then on, people would be able to travel great distances in relative comfort and in very little time! They would now be able to look at the world as only the birds had, until that point in history! Today, we are no longer excited over the airplane, but relate to it as commonplace. The same applies to the telephone, car, refrigerator, computer and tape recorder. If someone who lived several generations ago would come back to life in our times, he would be *stunned* at the achievements that were beyond imagination in his day. At most, today, we may be excited temporarily when someone first markets a more sophisticated gadget.

Conclusion

Natural and technological miracles surround us constantly. However, we do not pay attention to them at all. Someone who can imagine how he would have felt in the *absence* of this good, will be able to feel great joy in its presence. This awareness enables one to be happy that HaShem gives him life and strength, nourishment, clothes to keep him warm, and more and more. He comes to appreciate everything, and his joy is without bounds!

We have to wake up from the slumber of taking things for granted so that we may be content with our lot, and thank HaShem, Blessed be He, Who has granted us kindness without end. He has given us the intelligence to experience the wonders of creation and to invent new innovations for our benefit.

How can a person feel happiness and enthusiasm over his blessings which are beyond count? First, through considering their value *as* they occur. Second, we should consider how much we would be lacking if we did not have them, and then receive them enthusiastically.

The sense of excitement has the power to make a person dance all day long in ecstasy, joy and happiness!

4

WHAT DO I HAVE TO BE HAPPY ABOUT?

The manifold benefits conferred upon us by Heaven fall within two categories: those which are for all mankind, and those which are parceled out by HaShem on an individual basis. Thus far we have discussed the universal benefits to mankind. Now we shall elaborate on the personal benefits: such as wealth, health and esteem.

Jewish happiness reflects the fact that every individual's life is unique. In addition, people's natural character traits and talents vary widely. Wealth, health, self-esteem and children determine the external form of one's life. The combination of these variables presents an almost unlimited number of permutations which shape one's life. It is a mitzvah, a positive obligation, to be satisfied with the particular set of circumstances which Heaven has decreed appropriate for one's needs. One is required to feel content with his lot every moment of his life. R. Chaim Vital writes (*Sha'arei Kedushah*, Section 1, Chapter 2): "[One should feel] content with his lot continuously, since everything that is decreed by Heaven is for the good."

Prelude to Appreciation —
Rights Vs. Blessings

Before we begin to pave the road toward achieving happiness with one's share in life, we wish to discuss a prerequisite to positive thinking — the general outlook of a person concerning the fulfillment of his desires.

There are two approaches to this issue: either we feel that we are *entitled* to what we have, or we feel *blessed* to have it. The first approach, which claims, "I have it coming to me" results in the attitude that anything we get is due us, and therefore, we feel it is legitimate to expect to receive everything we want. When we feel entitled to have our desires satisfied, it follows that we express our wishes as demands, as Eisav said to Yitzchak (*Bereshit* 27:31), "Father, get up!" Paradoxically, however, having these wishes fulfilled does not make us happy, since receiving what we want is only getting what we expect.

In contrast, by following the second approach to fulfilling one's desires, one understands that everything he has is an unearned *gift* from HaShem. We have done nothing to deserve His kindnesses, and we make no demands of anyone else, either. With this attitude, compared to Eisav, Ya'akov asked his father to "Please get up..." (*Bereshit* 27:19). If HaShem has been gracious to us and fulfilled our desires and needs, we can be just as extraordinarily happy as if we have received a valuable, unexpected gift. Ya'akov expressed this feeling when he said (*Bereshit* 32:10), "I am too small for all of the kindness and righteousness which You have done for Your servant." With this perspective, if our desires do not materialize, we will not become angry or upset, as we did not feel entitled to have them fulfilled in the first place.

Appreciation

It is obligatory for each person to cultivate a deep sense of gratitude and appreciation for the countless benefits in his life. However, the daily trials and tribulations of life often blind the ability of a person to appreciate the benefits which are showered upon him. Therefore, one must *focus* his thoughts on the positive aspects of life, and take cognizance of the bounty of good that is his portion.

By appreciating the immense value of the things we already have, we can also appreciate the vast kindness HaShem does for us by giving them to us in the first place. Rather than seeking happiness from occasional occurrences, we can experience happiness in every aspect of our daily lives. By training ourselves not to take things for granted, we can ensure our constant happiness which emanates from the endless flow of precious gifts with which HaShem fills our lives.

Examples

As explained above, every human being is blessed in unique way. For example: one might be blessed with children. In order to appreciate this blessing one should sit separately with each child and see the attributes with which Hashem has blessed him so as to realize the uniqueness of each child — the cleverness of one, the devotion of the other, the creativeness of the third... Someone else might be blessed with a wonderful spouse. Spending time observing his or her special qualities and attitudes in common not only produces great satisfaction but also leads to a happy marriage! A third person might be blessed with good health — fortunate is he for whom the Creator has perfectly sustained the complex mechanism of his body.

Through these simple observations one can realize the great significance of his blessings and attain satisfaction.

Our Sages

Every human being is blessed with great wealth in one form or another. Let's consider the attitudes of our Sages which can help us "clear our glasses" so we can better realize what we actually have.

The *Gemara* (*Shabbos* 25b) quotes a halachic dispute of the *Tanaim*:

> "[Rabbi Meir says:] Who is a rich man? The one who is content with his wealth. Rabbi Tarfon says: The one who possesses a hundred vineyards and a hundred fields and a hundred servants to work in them [to do the necessary work in the fields — Rashi]. Rabbi Akiva says: The one who has a wife that is beautiful in her deeds. Rabbi Yossi says: The one who has a toilet close to his table."

We need an explanation as to what lies behind these seemingly odd statements of the *Tanaim*. Furthermore, on the surface, it appears that the opinion of Rabbi Meir is exactly that of the *mishna* in Avot: "Who is considered a wealthy person? He who is happy with his lot." Why then do the other *Tanaim* seem to oppose him, saying that wealth is dependent on specific material possessions? Is a person who does not have these material belongings free from the mitzvah of being happy with his lot?

From the commentary of *MaHaRitz Chayot* on the *Gemara*, it soon becomes clear that there is no dispute at all. The *Tanaim* agree that the definition of wealth is happiness with one's share, be it large or small. However, the Sages in our *mishna* were teaching us how they fulfilled this mitzvah in practice! Every *Tana* found something specific in his private life, through which he considered himself wealthy.

Rabbi Meir says: "Who is considered a rich man? He who finds satisfaction in his wealth."

Rabbi Meir earned his livelihood as a scribe, and barely made a living. He earned three *selaim* weekly. One he would spend on food, another on clothing, and the third *sela* he would contribute to Torah scholars (*Eruvin* 13a, *Gittin* 67a). Although his sustenance came to him with great difficulty, he felt satisfaction in his "wealth," and he lacked nothing.

Rabbi Tarfon says: "The one who owns a hundred vineyards and a hundred fields and a hundred servants to work them."

Rabbi Tarfon was an affluent man (as we learn in *Nedarim* 62a), and he actually owned fields and servants. But this, too, is a trial: not to aspire to *continue* increasing his assets and possessions without limit.

Rabbi Akiva says: "The one who has a wife that is beautiful in her deeds."

At the outset of his career, Rabbi Akiva was an extremely poor man, even more impoverished than Rabbi Meir. The *Gemara* (*Nedarim* 50a) relates that Rabbi Akiva's wife was the daughter of Kalba Savua, one of the wealthiest people in Jerusalem. Her father did not agree to the marriage, and therefore refused to support her and severed his relationship with her. "Rabbi Akiva and Rachel were married in the winter, and did not even possess anything to cover themselves with. They lived in a barn, and kept themselves warm with the hay." Yet despite his extreme poverty, Rabbi Akiva found something that made him feel rich and happy. It was his wife Rachel, who was "beautiful in her deeds." He did not merely settle for what he had, but was very content with his lot.

This explains the *Gemara* further: "Rabbi Akiva would pick the straw from her hair. He would say to her, 'If I had the ability, I would buy you a Jerusalem of Gold.' (a piece of gold jewelry on which the city, or the name, of Jerusalem was engraved.) Indeed, years later when his economic situation improved, Rabbi Akiva fulfilled his promise to his wife. Yet in his time of absolute poverty and economic distress, without any material possessions whatsoever, Rabbi Akiva was happy with his good fortune. He thought of the spiritual merits of his wife, and was therefore happy with the great wealth that was given him.

Rabbi Yossi says: "The one who has a toilet close to his table."

Rabbi Yossi is of the opinion that even if a person does not find anything to be happy about, he should find joy over the fact that he is healthy and does not suffer from ailments and pain. (The matter of the toilet in relation to health is explained in *Nedarim* 49b.)

The *Gemara* teaches us that no situation exists in which a

person cannot consider himself rich. Our Sages taught us by personal example, how, in the most difficult situations, they found reasons to be happy and joyful.

A Happy Marriage

The *Gemara* relates (*Yevamot* 63a): "Rabbi Chiya's wife would cause him anguish. [But] whenever he found something that she liked, he would bring it to her as a gift. Rav asked him, 'Why do you [go out of your way to] respect her while she is causing you sadness?' Rabbi Chiya answered, 'It is extremely important to appreciate what our wives are doing for us, by raising our children and saving us from sin.'"

How great are the deeds of Chiya! In spite of the grief that his wife caused him, he loved and respected her. He always considered her merits and ignored her faults. If all married couples would follow the example of Rabbi Chiya, they would undoubtedly be happy forever!

Rav Yehuda

The *Gemara* relates further (*Nedarim* 49b): Rav Yehuda's wife bought some wool and made a simple robe out of it. She would wear it whenever she went out to the market, and Rav Yehuda would wear it whenever he went to the synagogue. Due to this sharing arrangement, Rav Yehuda was once unable to attend an important meeting, as he did not have a proper garment to wear. Yet this incident did not make him sad. On the contrary, from that time, whenever he wore the robe, he recited a special *berachah*: "*Boruch*...who covers me with a coat". In another instance, Rav Yehuda was seen in his typical joyous mood, and was asked the reason. He answered that he was happy because he learned Torah. Rav Yehuda totally ignored his economic distress to such an extent that to an onlooker, he appeared to be a very rich man.

Reb Zusha

Reb Zusha of Anipoli (d. 1800) was a happy man who never worried, although he was sickly and lived in extreme poverty. He never knew where his next meal would come from, yet he lived with the simple faith that everything and anything is in the hands of *HaKadosh Boruch Hu* and he accepted everything with great equanimity and happiness.

A poor man once came to the Ba'al Shem Tov's great disciple, the Maggid of Mezritch, to ask how to achieve contentment with very little. The Maggid sent him to Reb Zusha to learn the virtue of *Histapkut* (contentment with the minimum). The man traveled a great distance and finally reached Reb Zusha. When he told him the purpose of his coming, Reb Zusha smiled apologetically and said, "I am terribly sorry that you went through all that trouble, but I'm afraid you came to the wrong person! I always have what I need and never lack anything. To learn how to be content with little, you have to go to someone who is poor...." The man returned and related to the Chassidim: "I learned not only how not to complain about having very little, but also how to be very happy with it!"

Reb Shalom Schwadron, Shlita (quoted in *The Maggid Speaks*, p. 56), relates that Reb Zusha would visit his Rebbe, the Maggid of Mezritch, from time to time. One day, before departing for his visit to the Rebbe, his wife reminded him of an important matter: "Several times I have asked you to ask for a *berachah* from the Maggid for our daughter who is

of marriageable age. You always forget. Please, try to remember this time!" Reb Zusha promised he would, and
went on his journey.

When he came to the Maggid, he told his Rebbe about
many problems and requests of others, but again ignored
his own personal problem. Before taking leave, the Maggid
said to him, "Is it true that you have a daughter to marry
off?" "Yes, indeed, but I forgot," Reb Zusha answered. The
Maggid gave him 300 Rubles and a *berachah* for success.

On his way home, Reb Zusha came into a wedding hall
where he noticed a great deal of tension and anxiety. He
learned that the mother of the bride was a widow and the
bride an orphan. The mother had saved 300 rubles which
she promised as a dowry, but the money had somehow
been lost and the wedding was about to be canceled. The
widow and the orphan in the bridal gown were both in
tears, and their grief and shame were too much for Reb
Zusha to bear. Suddenly everyone in the room heard the
stranger announce with great joy: "I found the money!"
and he handed over to the mother of the bride the 300
rubles intended for his own daughter. His reliance on
HaShem was so complete, that he was unconcerned as to
where he would get the money to marry his own daughter.
On the contrary, he had great simcha for the privilege of
fulfilling the important mitzvah of *Hachnassat Kallah*.

Had Reb Zusha lived a different kind of life, not being
content with the minimum of material means, he would
never have been able to sacrifice the dowry of his own
daughter and give it to someone else. But as he was always
happy with what he had, he was able to fulfill a great mitzvah without feeling that he was deprived of anything.

Conclusion

We see how the Sages and the Torah "greats" of all times were happy with their lot in every situation. We can compare their example with our circumstances which are far more comfortable, and recognize the great wealth which has been given to us. By focusing our thoughts on our many assets, we can be happy with our own lot. If we only reflect and observe, we will always find reason for Simchah.

"Don't Look Up!"

It is clear that in order to be happy, we need to focus on how well-off we already are. But like so many worthy goals, this is easier said than done. Too often, the heart does not listen to what the head already knows. We can understand intellectually that we are really well-off, but in our hearts we still feel deprived. How then, can we retrain our feelings?

Rabbeinu Bechaye (*Chovot HaLevavot, Avodat Elokim 7, Tafkid* 8) writes:

> "One should always keep one's eye on those
> who have fewer benefits in life, and not on
> those who have more."

The commentators explain that when you look at those who are better off than you are, you notice only what you are missing. It is like looking at the empty half of the cup. This naturally makes a person unhappy. Even if you eventually attain all of the honor and wealth you desire, as long as you keep looking at those who have more than you, you will continue to be unhappy. No one ever has more than *everyone* else of everything and by focusing on what you are missing, you disregard the good that you already have.

In contrast, if you "do not look up" at those who are better off than you are, but rather, "look down" at those who are worse off than you are, your attitude will improve immediately, since you will only see the things which you already have. Through this perspective, you will be struck by the many benefits you *do* have which other people are missing. You will then be able to enjoy the full half of your cup, so to speak, because regardless of how little you have, you will feel fortunate for having it.

This is the secret of how to feel happy and fulfilled all the time. If you are cold, you can console yourself with how much warmer you are than those who live in colder climates or who cannot afford such clothing or heat as you have. When you are hot, you can be happy that at least you are not cold or feverish. Should you fall sick, G-d forbid, there will surely be worse diseases to be grateful for being spared or worse cases of the illness you are suffering. Ultimately, one can feel happy he or she is alive.

Even one who falls prey to his evil inclination, has no reason to give up hope, for he is a *Jew*, instilled with a holy soul which can uplift him from all pitfalls!

Rabbi Akiva

Let's return to the story of Rabbi Akiva and Rachel which we referred to previously. The *Gemara* writes (*Nedarim* 50a) that when Kalba Savua found out about (the future Rabbi) Akiva's marriage to his daughter Rachel, he swore that she would never enjoy even a penny of his wealth. When Rabbi Akiva married Rachel it was winter, but they had no mattresses or blankets, and had to sleep on straw. Shortly after their marriage, the prophet Eliyahu came to them in the guise of a poor man and asked them for some of that very straw. He explained that his wife had just given birth, and they did not even have straw with which to warm themselves. Akiva's reaction was to say to Rachel, "You see — here is a man who does not even have straw!" Rachel responded, "In that case, I want you to go learn in a yeshiva."

The Ran explains that the prophet Eliyahu Hanavi did this in order to encourage Rachel and Rabbi Akiva. He brought to their attention that there were people even poorer than they were.

Rav Chaim Shmulevitz, Ztz"l, (*Sichot Mussar* 5733, *Ma'amar* 10), exposes the remarkable moral in this story. He writes: "Human nature is such, that when a man sees someone richer than himself, he feels himself lacking, and this lack upsets him. The main reason for this is that once a man sees that his fellow man has certain luxuries, the luxuries start to seem like necessities to him. In truth, to serve HaShem the right way, you must look at those *poorer* than yourself. Then you will feel HaShem's goodness, and you will not consider your situation to be lacking in anything. After all, in this world, everything is measured *in relative terms*, by comparing what one has *in relation to others*. Rabbi Akiva and his wife learned this lesson from Eliyahu, who comforted them and gave them peace of mind from worry over what they lacked. With this realization, Rachel was able to say, 'Go straight to the house of a rav,' since if we are not lacking any necessities, you have no license not to study Torah. It was this determination which produced Rabbi Akiva."

In the Vale of Death

A survivor of the Holocaust disclosed that it was just this approach which helped her survive the terrors of the War. Her father had taught her to always think about those who were in more dire straits than they were. She was the daughter of a well-to-do family and had enjoyed every material comfort before the War. When the War broke out, she and her entire family were left penniless. What is more, they had to flee from place to place with the fear of death continually hovering over them. Yet in spite of this terrible ordeal, even in the most difficult of situations, she was able to remain strong and did not despair. She always imagined the plight of those who were worse off than she, and she was grateful to at least be alive. This thought helped her to overcome all the dangers that continually threatened her. Time after time she found the courage and strength to find some resource by which to save herself from her persecutors, until she was finally saved from the vale of death and could begin a new life.

Learning from Our Past

History has so much to teach us in this realm. There have been few, if any, generations as rich in material goods and comforts as ours. The poorest among us is better off than the average Jew of only two generations ago. If we could only remember the terrible straits that the residents of Jerusalem suffered fifty or a hundred years ago; the monstrous travails of the generation that endured the War; the oppression of the Jews of the Soviet Union, and many more similar examples, we would be able to appreciate the good that HaShem has done for us individually and as a generation. We would forget all the things we are supposedly lacking which, after all, are insignificant compared to the hardships which our fathers and grandfathers endured.

Simchah in Times of Trouble

Aside from what we have discussed, that one's troubles can be diminished by comparing them with the plight of others, there is a more absolute, profound perspective which Judaism offers us. Even when trouble befalls a person, without any visible ray of hope to illuminate the darkness or to give him reason for happiness, he must still have complete faith in HaShem that this, too, is for his good.

> "Rav Yitzchak said: A person was going from place to place, and saw a mansion on fire. Said the man, 'Is it possible that this mansion is without a leader (owner)?' The owner of the mansion looked at him and said, 'I am the owner of the house.' So it is regarding Avraham Avinu, who said, 'Could it be that this world is without a leader?' *HaKadosh Boruch Hu* revealed Himself to Avraham and said, 'I am the Sovereign of the world.' " (*Yalkut, Bereshit* 12)

One who observes the wondrous order and marvels of Creation and the Divine Providence in everyday life, will come to see very clearly, that there is a supernatural Force that leads, directs and supervises the entire universe. If at times it seems to us that something most unfortunate is taking place, we must strengthen our faith and our conviction that the "manager" dwells above, observes all matters, and ultimately brings everything toward a conclusion that is good.

The following are several examples to illustrate the fact that by the grace of HaShem, salvation actually stems from the trouble itself and that out of the darkness itself springs forth light. From these, we may draw the strength and the courage to never give up hope and to relate to every situation in life, even the most oppressive ones, in a positive manner.

Back to the Land of Egypt

After the exit of the Children of Israel from Egypt, HaShem suddenly commanded them to retreat: "Speak to the Children of Israel that they return and camp in front of Pi HaChirot" (*Shemot* 14:2). Rashi comments: "They shall go backwards, in the direction of Egypt." The Ibn Ezra comments: "Truthfully, the intelligent person should not think about 'why HaShem did do so', for all His deeds are with plan and purpose, and the wisdom of man is like nothingness compared to His wisdom. I mention this so that one should take note that it was with intentional wisdom that HaShem commanded them to return backwards, in order that Pharaoh should go out and run after them, and drown in the sea.... The thoughts of HaShem are profound!"

The Selling of Yosef

At the time that it happened, the selling of Yosef seemed a terrible tragedy. Yet years later, this very event made possible Yosef's ascent to the royal government, giving him the ability to support his father and brothers. In the words of the verse, (*Bereshit* 45:7): "HaShem sent me before you to save your lives through a great deliverance."

Rabbi Akiva

Said Rabbi Akiva, "A person should always be in the habit of saying: 'All that the Merciful One does, He does for the good.' "

Once Rabbi Akiva went on a journey and came to a certain township. He asked for a place to stay overnight, and they refused him. Rabbi Akiva said (*Berachot* 60b): "All that the Merciful One does, He does for the good." And he went and slept in the field. He had with him a rooster, a donkey and a candle. Along came the wind and blew out the candle; a cat came and ate the rooster; a lion came and ate the donkey. Said Rabbi Akiva, "All that the Merciful One does, He does for the good." That same night a Roman garrison captured the town and took all the inhabitants captive. Said Rabbi Akiva, "Did I say that HaShem does everything for the good?"

Rashi comments that, "Had the candle been burning, the Roman soldiers would have noticed Rabbi Akiva; had the donkey brayed or the rooster crowed, the Romans would have heard them and captured him, too."

Rabbi Yehoshua ben Levi

The *Yalkut MeAm Loez* (*Bamidbar*) brings an awesome story about Rabbi Yehoshua ben Levi who met Eliyahu the Prophet: Rabbi Yehoshua prayed before HaShem to fulfill his wish and his prayer was answered and his wish granted — Eliyahu HaNavi revealed himself to him. Eliyahu asked him, "What do you request?" Rabbi Yehoshua answered, "I want to watch what you do in this world." "This is impossible" answered Eliyahu. "Why?" asked Rabbi Yehoshua. "Because you will see me do things that you will not be able to bear." "I do not care, I wish to go with you." "Very well, come along with me," the prophet answered.

They went out together, and when it became dark, they found lodging with a poor couple who had nothing but a small cow. The poor man treated them well and offered them food, and honored them appropriately. At midnight Eliyahu rose and smote the cow on its head till it died. When Rabbi Yehoshua saw this, he cried and pleaded, "G-d forbid! This cannot be Eliyahu HaNavi; even a mountain robber would not do such a thing!" Turning to Eliyahu, he asked, "Is it not a sin, what you have done? This cow is the entire livelihood of this poor man, and you killed it! Is this the way to reciprocate the hospitality, the food and the majestic honor that he gave us?" Eliyahu answered him, "If you ask me once more, I shall part ways from you. If you wish to continue following me, be quiet and do not ask me any questions about the things I do."

They continued on their way, and on the second night they approached a rich man who was busy building his house. When the man saw them, he did not even take notice and went about his business. Neither did he offer them anything to eat or drink. At midnight Eliyahu rose, took a measuring rope by its end and ordered his companion to hold the rope by its other end. They took measurements, and Eliyahu built the host a beautiful mansion with a hundred and eighty rooms.

Rabbi Yehoshua was astonished. "The poor man gave us

food and shelter and accepted us with great honor, and you killed his cow. Yet for the rich man who did not even welcome you properly, you perform such a miracle and build him a large palace worth a fortune?!"

From there they traveled to a place where all the inhabitants were affluent people. They were so arrogant that they did not even *look* at the two learned rabbis, much less offer them any hospitality. In the morning Eliyahu HaNavi prayed that they should all become leaders.

From there they journeyed to a different place, where all the people were poor. When these people saw the two guests, they accepted them with great honor and offered them food and drink in spite of their poverty. On the next day Eliyahu beseeched HaShem that they should not have more than one leader.

At this, Rabbi Yehoshua Ben Levi cried to Eliyahu: "I can take no more! Please explain the reasons behind your deeds, for I do not understand them at all!"

Eliyahu answered, "If I explain it all to you, you cannot come with me any more."

Said Rabbi Yehoshua, "I agree to everything, as long as you give me an explanation of what has taken place. Why did you kill that poor man's cow?"

The Prophet answered: "On that particular night, the wife of the poor man was about to die. She was dearer to him than all the gold in the land. Therefore, I killed their cow to atone for the woman, 'a soul instead of a soul.' "

Rabbi Yehoshua demanded further, "And why did you build a large mansion for that rich man who did not offer us anything to eat or drink?"

Answered Eliyahu, "Be informed that had this man dug two or three cubits into the ground under the house, he would have found a great treasure. Therefore, I built the mansion. That mansion will not last long, because it is built by miraculous means. It will collapse suddenly without revealing the treasure."

"And why did you bless those affluent people that they should all turn into leaders?" asked Rabbi Yehoshua.

"It is not a blessing but a curse, for too many leaders bring destruction. As people say, 'Too many captains sink the ship.' But those poor people who were hospitable to us, I blessed them that they should have only one leader, because a place that has only one leader will endure. In the words of Ben Sira: 'In the hands of an understanding man, the city will be peaceful.' If you see a wicked man who is serene and relies on his wealth, you should know that it is not to his benefit. And if you see a righteous man who suffers anguish and need, it is not to his disadvantage but for his good, to atone for his soul."

Conclusion

The lesson to be drawn from these stories is that the human mind cannot grasp the plan and purpose of the Divine Wisdom behind the circumstances and events of our lives.

We see, therefore, that there is nothing in the world about which one can be absolutely certain, no matter how bad it may seem. It is our task to be confident, always, that the "Manager of the house," *HaKadosh Baruch Hu*, guides all events so that everything turns out for the best: "The stone which the builders refused, has become the headstone of the corner. This is HaShem's doing; it is marvelous in our eyes (Psalms 118)."

5

EXPANSIONISM

Lack of Contentment

After discussing the method and attitudes which enable us to achieve happiness, we are now ready to consider the negative traits — expansionism (greed) and competition — which nullify the effectiveness of what we have discussed above.

Discontent is the most common cause of unhappiness and people will display dissatisfaction with every imaginable situation in life - such as inadequate income, poor social status, lack of talents and even the weather.

Before steps can be taken to increase happiness, one must first learn to stop *creating* unhappiness as a result of the things one *imagines* he lacks. There are many different causes of discontent, and we will look at them one by one.

Greed

Rabbeinu Bechaye (*Chovot HaLevavot, Sha'ar HaBechinah*) writes:

"[Because of] people's preoccupation with worldliness and its pleasures, and their greed for worldly goods, their hearts are filled with the hope that they will fulfill these desires, and in this pursuit they completely neglect to consider the benefits the Creator bestows upon them. Once they reach the fulfillment of their [worldly] needs, they immediately create new goals to attain additional material possessions. Consequently, His many benefits to them seem few in their eyes, and His great gifts are diminished by them...."

People who are caught up in the race for worldly possessions and pleasures do not take the time to appreciate their gains and achievements, since the moment they achieve one desire, they begin to yearn for the next one.

The Gaon Rav E. E. Dessler (*Michtav Me'Eliyahu* I, p. 41) has a profound explanation for the force which drives a person to enter this endless chase for worldly, and often worthless, attainments:

"Aspiration is a force which attracts a person to desire things which seem to be unattainable. It is different from physical hunger, which is a limited need to fill one's stomach. In contrast, one who falls prey to the desire for wealth or the like does not wish for something limited, but rather, is ruled by a constant driving force *to expand his boundaries*, to continually possess new things which are beyond himself *just because they are outside his reach*. Therefore, it is not because of the importance of the things themselves that he desires to have them, but only because he feels that they are outside his realm.

This does not apply only to the love of money. It is true for all material desires as well. For example, the *Gemara* (end of *Nedarim*) discusses [this concept in relation to] the case of a suspected adulterer who is hiding in a house when the husband returns home to eat his dinner. The husband is about to eat something poisoned by a snake, when suddenly the [suspected] adulterer cries out and saves him.

Rava states that there is no concern that such a person is truly an adulterer, since if he were, he would have let the husband die. However, the *Gemara* asks, why do we state the obvious? Rather, one could say that [the suspect actually] is an adulterer, and that he prefers the husband to live so that the wife will continue to be forbidden to him and therefore be more desirable (as in "stolen waters taste sweet").

Although the *Gemara* rejects this line of argument, one still wonders — is it not a plausible possibility? In answer, Tosafot explains that an adulterer does not know the concept of forbidden fruits being more desirable because they are forbidden. This explanation is not self-evident, however, and still needs clarification.

[R' Dessler continues that] the matter can be understood in light of our discussion above. A person who covets *is not aware* that his craving comes from the fact that the object he longs for is withheld from him. He does not realize that if he were to attain [his desire] in a permissible manner, its appeal would diminish and the pleasure it provides would be considerably reduced. Instead, he imagines that his entire future hinges on attaining this particular object itself, and that if he would possess it, he would be happy forever! If he knew how much of this notion is imaginary, he would no longer run after [his desires]."

Modern Innovations

Rav Dessler's principle is one of the fundamental concepts exploited by modern economics. The concept of "creating a need," as business strategy terms it, is nothing more than an approach to take advantage of this tendency. People desire *anything*, so long as it is something they do not already have. It is not necessarily true that inventions and modern technological innovations always supply the things that society needs, but once a new device or service becomes available, masses of people will be attracted by it, only because it is *new*, that is, something that until now has been *beyond them*. If necessity or usefulness were the true motive, the sales of less useful inventions would be lower. But, in fact, the reverse is true. The more farfetched the invention, the greater its power to sway the masses to buy it. Look at one of the most famous success stories in the history of marketing: the Pet Rock. A small, smooth rock in a decorative box, with instructions on how easy it is to care for this low maintenance "pet" — this *rip-off* sold millions!

The Pursuit of Wealth

Kohelet (Ecclesiastes 5:9) teaches that: "One who loves

money will be dissatisfied, no matter how much he has". *Chazal* (our Sages) (*Chulin* 46a) also tell us: "The rich are tight-fisted." The Maharal (*Netiv HaOsher*, Ch. 2) questions why these statements, which seem to defy common sense, are true. He explains that *kessef* "money," is a derivative of *kossef*, "longing," since for a rich person money is always a longing. He is never satisfied by it, even for a moment.

We can understand this to be rooted in the phenomenon, described by Rav Dessler above: that people are driven to pursue the attainment of material possessions which are presently beyond their reach. The happiness one feels in having money or wealth is based on its unlimited *potential* for providing pleasure. That is why a rich person hates to spend money, even for his own necessities. This avarice has no limit, by definition, since it is a desire to have *the potential* to acquire more than what one now has. Therefore, there can never be any satiety in money, or any other material acquisitions — only an endless longing.

The Pursuit of Pleasure

Expansionism takes its toll on most of us. If riches are not our dream, then some other worldly desire is probably taking its place. Even if our days are not preoccupied with trying to gain material benefits, we treat each physical pleasure as if *more* of it will surely provide true happiness. When we have an item in hand, our imagination not only inflates the amount of pleasure it can afford us, but our minds immediately race forward to fantasize how much greater the *next* source of pleasure will be. With this attitude, we tend to overlook the real pleasure the particular item at hand is actually providing for us. With every bite, we look forward to the forkful to come and ignore the flavor of what we have in our mouths at present. Since this tendency repeats itself on every occasion, it follows that we pay no more attention to the next bite, the next fulfilled wish, than we did to the previous bite (or fulfilled wish). No wonder that in retrospect so many people feel dissatisfied! At no point did they stop to savor their pleasures!

This is the pitiful situation referred to in the verse (Ecclesiastes 1:2): "Vanity of vanities, all is vanity." The fact that worldly pleasures are limited is clear enough. But what does the doubling of the word "vanity" signify? King Solomon is bemoaning the *double* waste involved in pursuing material things: not only is physical pleasure largely unsatisfying, but people do not even enjoy the pleasure that their worldly attainments afford them. Instead of enjoying their material benefits, they are busy dreaming of the imagined pleasures to come. This is "vanity *of* vanities"! (The vanity created from the vanity itself!)

Satisfaction

In light of these insights, we can now define a simple rule for relieving the discontent caused by expansionism. The rule is: train yourself to focus on how good the things are that you already have. Thus, you can find a wealth of pleasure and contentment *right there* at your fingertips.

Blessings

The Torah — our profound guidebook to achieving all

the positive character traits — incorporates in its mitzvot the ingredients for contentment. Let us consider two mitzvot: Blessings and Shabbat.

We have already discussed the benefits of reciting blessings *before* enjoying the many pleasures Hashem gives us. Now let us consider the merits of reciting blessings *after* we have enjoyed ourselves. Reciting a blessing after receiving various pleasures (e.g., after eating) *focuses* our attention on the benefits we have just received and thus we are more likely to realize that we *have* enjoyed them! This increases our overall daily pleasure, and protects us from the urge to pursue additional valueless goals, as if real happiness can be found "out there," beyond ourselves and what we already have. The root commandment of all such blessings is "You will eat and *be satisfied* and bless....", making satisfaction a necessary condition for blessing (*Berachot* 20b). Although it is certainly possible for a person to recite a blessing mechanically rather than to fulfill the requirement to *realize* his satisfaction first, the commandment to recite a blessing makes it more likely that we will take note of what is at hand and so, *have been* satisfied.

Shabbat — Full of Happiness

"On the *seventh* day HaShem completed His work which He had done, and He rested on the *seventh* day from all of His work which He had done" (*Bereshit* 2:2).

The Hebrew word for the number seven, *sheva*, derives from the word *sovei*, which means "replete", abundantly satisfied (Maharal). The seventh day, Shabbat, is the day of repletion, of *sevia*. On Shabbat, when one ceases material pursuits, he should feel a sense of completeness.

Shabbat was given solely to the Jewish people. In the *Shmonah Esrei* (Silent Prayer) of Shabbat, we describe the holy day: "HaShem, our G-d, You have not given it to the nations of the world and, our King, You have not bequeathed it to the idol worshippers, nor have the uncircumcised dwelt in His rest. But You have given it to Israel, Your nation, with love, to the seed of Ya'akov, whom You have chosen." Shabbat was given to the Jewish People so they can train themselves to rest from the pursuit of further pleasures and be happy with the things they already have.

This concept is explained by the Maharal (*Aguddat Shabbat* 30): "Shabbat [leads to] stopping and resting, for that is the meaning of the term *shovat* [the root of the word Shabbat]: it means resting and stopping. This is because Shabbat is a stopping and resting for the world, since on Shabbat the world rested."

Practical advice: To induce the feeling of contentment, one might want to list at the end of the week (before Shabbat), goals that have been accomplished during that week. Looking back and reviewing these accomplishments — on the day of rest — will notably increase the feeling of contentment.

Luxuries

The most common form of avarice is not the greed for money nor the desire for inaccessible physical pleasures, but rather, the craving for ever greater and fancier luxuries.

The pursuit of luxury leads to the follies that we have discussed. Firstly, luxuries are devoid of intrinsic worth and are therefore unable to provide real satisfaction. Secondly, they are by definition something *extra*, and therefore, as soon as one acquires a luxury he devalues its worth and gains little pleasure from it. After all — it is now no longer something extra! But the desire for luxury has a further dimension of folly. Not only does it not provide pleasure, but it very often leads to great suffering.

The Rambam writes (*Moreh Nevochim* III, 12) how, after getting accustomed to owning unnecessary things, people begin to actually desire luxuries. First they acquire sterling silverware, then gold flatware becomes the goal they work toward. But as gold is not the most beautiful material available, they soon find settings made of sapphire and rubies to which to aspire. No one, he explains, ever surpasses everyone else in luxuries.

Furthermore, observes the Rambam, the tragedy is that to acquire these unnecessary things, people will even endanger their health. The illnesses and injuries they may suffer as a consequence are then *self-inflicted*.

Actual necessities, the Rambam continues, are meant by G-d to be acquired with a *minimum of effort*. If something proves difficult to attain, it must be superfluous or luxuries must somehow be involved. In other words, even the basics can become impossible to reach if one has already exhausted oneself in the struggle for luxuries.

Rabbeinu Bechaye concurs with the Rambam on the deleterious effects of pursuing wealth. He comments on the verse (*Bereshit* 28:20): "Who has given me bread to eat and clothes to wear," — "This is what the righteous ask of HaShem. They do not ask for luxuries, but only for the basics without which one cannot live. Moreover, the tendency of men to seek out luxury is known to cause them a *great deal of hardship*."

Examples in Modern Life

If we could only take the Rambam's words to heart! By desiring only absolute necessities, we could save ourselves so much effort and suffering. The tension of planning and affording a wedding or a Bar-Mitzvah, for example, could be drastically reduced if the affair does not have to be super elegant. Many people grossly overreach their budgets for fear that hosting a simple dinner would cause them embarrassment. Others invest large amounts of time and strength in arranging the extravagant frills which seem appropriate to their financial standing. Both are mistaken; neither kind of sacrifice is necessary. In fact, people would enjoy their happy occasions more if they were less burdened and tired when the event took place.

Similarly, men, and even women with families, sometimes take on extra jobs to provide supplementary income for things which are not really necessary. Is the purported gain really worth the clear loss — the tension and pressure, the time sacrificed from home, wife and children?

There are endless examples of the Rambam's principle in everyday life. People bring trouble upon themselves in all sorts of ways. Besides material objects, there are also unnecessary situations and circumstances, such as job promotions, honorary positions, and so on, which people desire. In some instances, these can be considered luxuries, too. Rather than feeling deprived if you lack some wished-for

status, be grateful; you have been spared the bitter consequences which usually follow such ambitions. Certainly,
do not invest any effort in obtaining luxuries, since the
result is so often self-inflicted suffering.

The commentary *Pat Lechem* on the *Chovot HaLevavot*
(*Sha'ar HaBitachon*, Ch.4) discusses this principle in detail:
"In one's business matters, one should aim to acquire only
those worldly goods that are necessary for one's survival.
When HaShem sees fit to give one more than the bare es-
sentials, it will surely come about of its own accord, without one's worrying oneself or tiring oneself over it. Man's
nature truly craves a bit of leavening beyond the bare necessities, as shown by our blessing '...for everything that
You have created to sustain them with.' Still, a person
should not overly exert himself for [those extra benefits],
since it is not necessary. [Rather,] he should trust that
HaShem will give him a sense of satisfaction from the necessities he already has."

Summary

We have learned that the pursuit of wealth, worldly
pleasures and luxuries stems from the urge to *expand beyond*. This craving creates an endless hunger and is self-de-
feating, for it does not let the person feel contentment and
happiness with what he *has* achieved, and leads him to
unnecessary hardships. The Torah teaches us to curb this
craving and to be happy with what we have.

6

COMPETITION

Until now, we have discussed avarice, which is the craving for physical possessions and pleasures in and of themselves. As long as one desires to have material things in abundance, he can never be content. But as soon as one begins to tame one's avaricious desires, and strives to enjoy the simple pleasures that HaShem gives freely, one directly confronts an even stronger drive: the competitive urge — the desire to feel successful *in comparison*.

The Standards of Modern Society

The *Chovot HaLevavot* has written (*Sha'ar HaPrishah*, Ch. 2):

> "As the world becomes ever more sophisticated, the destruction becomes ever greater; evil ways become good in men's eyes. They make them into laws and morals, and they pass them on from father to son. Every peculiar thing in the world seems reasonable to

them, the proper approach — of making do with little — they consider peculiar; the refraining from luxuries, they see as a failure to fulfill one's duty, and everyone copies whatever his fellow man does. One who enjoys only as much as he needs of this world is called lazy, and one who refrains from acquiring more possessions than necessary is considered weak and pitiful. One who chases after luxuries is thought industrious, however, and by their material possessions, they glorify themselves and think themselves great. They make their stomachs into a god; their clothing into their torah, and the improvement of their homes, their morality."

The *Chovot HaLevavot* describes the labels that society gives those who do not strive for material success. And as he implies, even those who do not believe in these labels still succumb to their negative effects. Poor people are not only considered inferior by others, but they generally feel inferior themselves. Those who are not climbing the conventional ladder of success usually feel as peculiar as they are thought to be. Many a person who feels satisfied with his standard of living will strive to raise it only to avoid the pity or derision of his fellow man.

Honor

The Ramchal (*Mesilat Yesharim* Ch. 11) calls the drive behind this world-wide competition by its true name:

"*Honor* drives the heart of man more than all of the urges and desires in the world. If not for [honor], a man would be content to eat whatever he eats, to wear whatever covers his nakedness, to live in any home which protects him from the elements. Earning his livelihood would be easy for him, and he would not have to exert himself to get rich. But in order not to see himself lower than his fellowmen, he engages in this undertaking, and there is no end to his labor."

The Ramchal reveals here, that the main factor in a person's sense of discontent with his material status is his desire for honor in comparison with his fellowman. The feeling that he is missing something in life is actually a concern that he is missing something that will elevate him in the eyes of others. Rather than focusing on the value of the things which he already has and on the use and enjoyment that he can gain from his possessions, such a person discounts his present financial standing, considering it nothing more than a stepping stone for social betterment. But when everyone uses wealth to prove his superiority over everyone else, obviously the social pressure can only spiral in intensity.

Salvation

How can a person maintain values opposed to those of everyone around him? How can one protect himself from the feelings of inferiority that society imposes on those who refuse to accumulate wealth? The only salvation is to drive it into one's consciousness: material success is *a completely meaningless idol*. No matter how ardently financial status is worshipped by society, it is absolutely false as an ideal.

Yet can one really free himself completely of all envy, comparison and competition with his fellows?

We have seen that it is honor which is at the root of society's race for luxuries and financial standing. But if instead, one cleaves to a concept of success which is based on *true* values, he can succeed in replacing the irrational, useless feelings of envy which society breeds. It is only when one is free of envy and foregos social competition that he can begin to be content with his lot. Contentment is a prerequisite for happiness. Unfortunately, by imagining social status as a key to happiness, the vast majority of people choose to join in the race for this false happiness, leaving true happiness further behind them the more they pursue this illusion.

Non-Material Competition

People's sense of discontent does not limit itself to the arena of material possessions. There are also those who forfeit their happiness by wishing for greater abilities: "winning personalities" or accomplishments in non-material fields. Greater intelligence, popularity, business sense, education and so on, are often imagined to be prerequisites for lasting happiness. Even a lack of spiritual attainments can lead one to unnecessary dissatisfaction, if one misunderstands the true nature of spiritual striving.

In such areas, it often seems that one can objectively evaluate whether one's situation is good or bad. A weak student for example, who repeatedly fails in his studies despite hard work, can be understood for feeling sorry for himself. Isn't his poor intelligence hard luck that he can do nothing about but become depressed? But as we will see, most of his misery is caused by his comparing himself with others. If he dealt only with the "bad" circumstance itself, he would be able to perceive that, not only is he not as unlucky as it seems, but that he has many unique qualities which he has overlooked, and which actually make him superior to others.

The way to avoid the negative tendency towards competition, is to reverse one's way of thinking. Instead of comparing one's faults to the qualities of others and becoming envious of them, one need only realize and concentrate on the attributes in which one excels, and take proper pride in them.

"One of a Kind" in His Own Eyes

Everyone, without exception, can find some area in which he excels over his fellow. One day, Rav Chaim Shmulevitz, Ztz"l, happened to see some sanitation workers collecting trash in their truck. Suddenly, one of the workers came over to the Rosh Yeshiva, who had been absorbed in his thoughts, and said to him self-importantly, "Rebbi, do you think that it's always this way, with him up on top and me on the bottom? In half an hour, you'll see that I'm on top and he's on the bottom!" After this incident, Rav Chaim delivered a talk in the yeshiva on the subject of self-respect, and he showed how everyone, in his own field, sees himself as "up on top" (From *Moach VaLev* 129).

When a person uses his feelings of self-respect to develop his own unique abilities (but not to act superior to his fellows, of course), he can reach the highest levels.

Trade/Profession

Everyone is unique and special in his own way. Let us take for example a person's trade/profession. HaShem has granted everyone special talents to enable him to support himself. The *Gemara* says (*Berachot* 43): Rav asked, "What [do the words of the verse,] 'He has made everything beautiful in its time' mean? It teaches that HaShem has made each individual's trade attractive to him." Rashi explains: "Even a tanner [whose livelihood carries with it a particularly obnoxious smell] finds his work pleasing. HaShem made it so, so that the world would not be missing any trade." This means that everyone is blessed with his own special talents, and that anyone who cultivates his innate potential can find happiness and self-respect. The feeling of self-respect is implanted in people's hearts by a special providence from *HaKadosh Baruch Hu*, in order to make the world complete.

Even so, it sometimes happens that a person tries, for whatever reasons, to work in a field for which HaShem has given him no talent and of course he is not successful. Instead of despairing, he should consider an occupation which *does* take advantage of the abilities that have been given to him, rather than trying to work at a trade he had originally considered more respectable. If a trade or profession does not suit him, he should search for and develop the unique talents HaShem has instilled in him, in order to be worthy of His blessings.

Contentment with One's Spiritual Progress

Of all the non-material pursuits, spiritual attainments are the most important. Therefore, failing to realize one's spiritual goals can lead to the greatest unhappiness. However, what often happens is that people feel dissatisfied with their spiritual accomplishments, not because they have none, but because they do not appreciate the significance of what they *have* attained. They look at the great men of their generation and conclude that any spiritual level short of what these individuals have achieved is not of value. By so doing, however, they set themselves up for a lifetime of self-denigration and dissatisfaction.

The solution, in this case, is perfectly simple. One must constrict his field of comparison to himself alone. In such a state, every improvement in one's spiritual level can make him very happy. Without an outside standard of comparison, a person has no reason to consider his achievements insignificant.

This may seem to be a way of fooling oneself, or of allowing oneself to settle for lesser accomplishments, but in fact this is actually the proper way to view our lives. Especially in spiritual matters, each person lives only his own life, with his own strengths and abilities, and no man is obligated to achieve anything more than his own abilities allow. One does not have any reason to compete with one's fellows. In fact, in both spiritual and in many mundane matters, it is not only a mistake to do so, but is morally wrong.

It is told (in the commentary, *Brit Olam*, Introduction to *Sefer Chassidim*) about the saintly Rav Chaim Vital, Ztz"l, who asked his rebbe, the Ari Z"l, "In the *Talmud* and *Ris*-

honim we see that the good deeds, character and holiness of the early Sages were astounding. How can it be that no one in our generation can do even a thousandth of what they used to do?" The Rav answered, "Nowadays, the *yetzer hara* has become very powerful. Still, the little that one does today is just as precious to HaShem as the great deeds which the early Sages used to do!"

The *Midrash Rabbah* (*Bamidbar* 34:1) state:

> "HaKadosh Baruch Hu does not overburden His creatures. He expects of each individual only that which he is able. You find, when HaKadosh Baruch Hu gave the Torah to Yisrael, that had He come to them with the full strength of His power, they would not have been able to withstand it, as it says (Devarim 5), 'If we continue to hear....' Instead, He came to them only to the extent that they could bear it, as it says (Tehillim 29), 'The voice of HaShem is in strength.' The verse does not say, 'in His strength,' but only 'in strength.' That is, according to each and every one's strength."

The *Midrash Tanchuma* adds (*Shemot* 25), "Take note of how [HaShem's] voice was sounded for Yisrael: so that each one heard according to his strength. The elderly heard the voice according to their strength, young men according to theirs, grown boys according to theirs, children according to theirs, infants according to theirs, and women according to their strength. Even Moshe [heard it] according to his own strength."

HaKadosh Baruch Hu has granted specific strengths to each individual, according to His Divine understanding and wisdom, which have no end. Thus, each person's service of HaShem must be accomplished through utilizing specifically those abilities which he has been granted. It is for this reason that the *Gemara* (*Berachot* 5b) is able to say that one need not be sorry if he has not learned a great amount of Torah, since we learn that "one who accomplishes much and one who accomplishes little are equal, as long as they dedicate their hearts to Heaven."

Spiritual Self-Sufficiency

In fact, the situation is even better than the above makes it seem. It is not just that one is exempt from attaining spiritual levels that he has not been given the tools to reach. In truth, anyone who tries to build his personality with those abilities that HaShem has given him will find that he *is* able to reach perfection, through these very abilities! He will be able to do without the advantages which seem necessary for other people to reach perfection.

This secret was revealed to us by the saintly scholar, Rav Yerucham, Ztz"l, of Mir, (*Da'at Chachmah U'Mussar* II, *Ma'amar* 55). He relates a conversation that occurred one Purim, between Rav Naftali Amsterdam, Ztz"l, and Rav Yisrael Salanter:

"Rebbi," said Rav Naftali, "If only I had the Rebbi's character, the heart of the [author of the] *Yesod VeShoresh HaAvodah*, and the head of the *Sha'agas Aryeh* — then I would be able...".

"Naftali!" Rav Yisrael answered him, "With *your* head, *your* heart and *your* character...."

Similarly, Rav Yerucham writes how Rav Shlomole Fein

(author of the *Leshem*), who was already known as a *Mekub-bal* (master of Judaism's mystical teachings) in his youth, once traveled with Rav Yisrael, Ztz"l. At last he found the courage to ask the great Rav why he did not learn *Kabbalah*. Rav Yisrael answered him, "Why do I need to know in which sphere *HaKadosh Baruch Hu* sits? I know one thing: that they will hit me with rods and it will hurt very much, and the beatings will 'burn.' This I know very well. Therefore, what else [do I need to know]?!"

Rav Yerucham explains "Everyone is obligated to use his own [abilities], and his own [abilities] are really everything he needs; he is not missing anything. 'With your own head and with your own character' — this fundamental teaching was revealed to us by the masters of *Mussar*."

According to this insight we can understand the above Midrash, that the Torah has been given equally to everyone, even though the ability to absorb it differs from one person to the next. One person may be blessed with a good memory and another with a keen intellect but each person, with his own abilities, can hear the same words of Torah from *HaKadosh Baruch Hu*, and can arrive at the same perfection: one person, mainly by means of his understanding of *Kabbalah*, another essentially by means of his understanding of *Mussar*, one with his heart, another with his brain. The author of the *Leshem* reached perfection by learning *Kabbalah*, and Rav Yisrael reached perfection by learning *Mussar*. One who truly accepts himself, with his own unique abilities and with his own strengths of character, can achieve everything.

The Gaon Rav Shlomo Wolbe writes at length about this principle in a letter to a young student (*Alei Shor* I, p. 37):

"How very strongly do I feel with you in your

anguish over your learning which 'doesn't go' ".... When you came to the yeshiva, perhaps you had exaggerated ideas about yourself and your talents. But then, each day, you saw more and more that the abilities that others have, you are lacking...until one day you had had as much as you could stand. You felt that you have nothing, neither talent, nor success, nor hope, but only weakness, misery, and distress. This feeling is called jealousy and envy. But let this be your consolation, my friend: all young people suffer from envy....

One who knows himself, knows his abilities, and knows what the Blessed Creator has granted him — has a great gift. One who takes advantage of his own strengths will attain every wished-for advantage, and achieve in the Holy Torah what the Creator of the world wanted him to achieve, and in the manner that the Creator of the world wanted him to achieve it. Such a person no longer suffers from jealousy.

But the young person who does not yet know himself and his character with a clear and honest understanding will look at himself with eyes that are not his own. He measures himself by the standards of his friends. He considers what he sees in his friends to be good and wants to be like them. Therefore, associating with those friends always puts him at the edge of his mental capabilities and talents, and he sees himself, not from within himself, but from the perimeter.

From there, he sees in himself more of the negative. This situation is described as "envy rots the bones." One who is infected with envy neglects the good and positive which HaShem has granted him, even to the point of his bones rotting. Only the advantages of others, his friends and his environment, are real advantages in his eyes....

Yes, *HaKadosh Baruch Hu*, Who prefers the Torah [over all else], gave you all the abilities you need in order for you to earn your portion in the Torah. Every morning, with great joy, you can recite the blessing '*She'asah li kol tzarki* — Who has provided my every need,' both in material things and in spiritual matters. 'Everything that I need to fulfill my purpose in the world, everything that I need to earn my portion in Torah, everything *HaShem Yitbarach* has given me!' "

Learning from a Baby

Babies are delighted with every step of their progress through the various stages of development: from lying on their backs to rolling over; from rolling to crawling, from crawling to walking. A baby feels that with each accomplishment, a new world has opened up for him, and this fills him with great happiness. But, if he were to look at his elders and compare his state to theirs, he would despair of ever progressing or developing. Since he looks only at himself, however, he is happy (according to *Chovot HaLevavot, Bechinah* 5). Happiness is the basis for a baby's progress.

As we have seen, the key to happiness is to avoid looking at those who are better off than you are. Learn from the infant not to look up to levels which are beyond you. There is never a need to consider other's material advantages, and even other people's spiritual accomplishments should be taken only as possible goals, not as a basis for negative comparisons. By properly appreciating the good that HaShem bestowed upon you, and by taking pride in whatever spiritual perfection you have attained, according to your own level, you will be able to feel true happiness, in every situation, all the time.

Conclusion

We have found that there are two basic characteristics which cause a person to be dissatisfied with his lot: desire — which causes a person to always desire whatever is beyond him (the characteristic of "stolen waters"); and honor — which drives a person to be superior to his fellow-man, causing him to find little satisfaction, neither with his income, his material goods, nor his spiritual attainments.

Rabbi Eliezer HaKapar said, "Envy, desire and honor take a person out of the world" (*Avot* 4:28). The world referred to in this saying is *this* world (not the World to Come), since these three characteristics bring a life of sorrow and of dissatisfaction with what one has!

Summary of Part One

As we have seen, happiness is an internal trait and an intrinsic virtue. Material goods and worldly success can contribute to a person's happiness to the extent that he properly values that which he has. Rather than chase luxuries, a man should learn to ignore the things which he does not have and feel grateful for that which he has been given.

The virtue of happiness is acquired like other virtues: slowly, and one step at a time. First, we have to train ourselves to observe and realize the value of the treasures with which we have been blessed — the personal blessings that every individual is fortunate to have, and the general blessings bestowed on all mankind. Second, we have to instill this attitude into ourselves, by way of excitement and enthusiasm. It takes work and a lot of patience, but we are capable of overcoming our irrational feelings. Soon, the momentary pleasures of this world will become dim shadows, compared to the steady, constant happiness that we will have acquired. "Who is a wealthy person? He who is happy with his lot" (*Avot* 4:1).

PART II

"ACTIVE SIMCHAH":

Cheerfulness and Joy

1

GROWING THROUGH SIMCHAH

Having considered the first, "passive" aspect of Simchah — contentment and satisfaction over one's lot, we are now ready to look at the second aspect — Active Simchah. To fully understand the concept of "Active Simchah," we must delve into the inner recesses of the soul, to comprehend the source from which Simchah emanates.

Man's Will

The Vilna Gaon writes (Proverbs 1:23):

> "For every action a man does, he receives a *ruach* (spiritual inspiration) from Heaven. This *ruach* does not rest until it performs other similar actions. It derives great pleasure from these actions, whether they be mitzvot or transgressions. This *ruach* is the source of man's will, and the will stems from this *ruach*."

Man's drive and will to realize his potential is one of his

most essential qualities. It is no coincidence that he is named Adam, which alludes to the perpetual drive of the Earth (*adama*) to grow and expand. Just as the earth nurtures the seeds and provides them with nourishment to grow forth, so, too, each individual aspires to develop the particular talents and traits which he feels are central to his existence. The Vilna Gaon illustrates this drive: "Just as the rider of a horse is able to steer his mount in the proper direction by means of strenuous efforts, even if the horse is wild and untamed, so, too, a person whose character is naturally evil may control his path in life. *Everything depends upon a person's will*" (*Even Shelemah* 1:5).

The Equilibrium between Simchah and Man's Will

The Vilna Gaon explains (Proverbs 18:14):

"Simchah stems from the *Ruach* [will]".

In the words of the Sabah of Kelm (*Chachma U'Mussar* II p. 172):

"The absence of Simchah is the absence of will [desire], for they are *one and the same.*"

Here is a marvelous revelation: That very will which we have described above, so essential for a person's development, is also the source of the virtue of Simchah! Thus, one can readily understand that this relationship between will and Simchah is the reason for the profound importance of Simchah in all aspects of life. Simchah nurtures a person's drive to grow and expand his horizons.

Let us continue examining the words of the Vilna Gaon (ibid.): "A person who is able to maintain a state of Simchah will become cured from disease; Simchah is capable of nullifying sickness. Conversely, a person in low spirits is incapable of recovering from disease."

The beneficial effects of Simchah are not limited to overcoming physical disease. They are felt in all aspects of one's life. A person who feels Simchah has the ability to overcome any obstacle in his path.

Says King Solomon, the Wisest of Wise (Proverbs 15:13): "A merry heart makes a cheerful countenance, and by sorrow of the heart, the spirit is broken." According to the Vilna Gaon (ibid.), this means: The cheerful face of a person bespeaks a will within his heart, evidence of his aspirations and of the destiny that he desires to reach. One who is happy at heart "has a cheerful countenance." His strong will drives him to translate his desires into action. In contrast, "by sorrow of the heart, the spirit is broken." The Vilna Gaon explains (ibid.): "For the desire of a person to do a mitzvah, or any other act, comes from the spirit that is within him. But the person whose heart is sorrowful, his spirit is broken. He is impatient and despises everything, and he is therefore totally inactive."

Simchah —
The Way to Overcome

Life is full of obstacles. From the moment a person is born, he is faced with all sorts of barriers which he must overcome. By maintaining a state of Simchah — the source of every Jew's ability to overcome all — a person can sustain an optimistic spirit.

It is told that one of the masters of Chassidism would agree to speak to people who committed transgressions, yet he would adamantly refuse to speak to people who felt low in spirit. He reasoned that as long as a person feels Simchah, there is still hope that he will overcome his Evil Inclination. Someone who experiences melancholy, however, cannot be helped out of his situation.

Similarly, there is a story about Rav Simchah Bunim of Danzig which illustrates this idea: Rav Simchah once saw a person drowning in the sea, and he called out to him, "Send my regards to the whale!" He then threw a plank of wood to the drowning man, who managed to hang on for dear life. Rav Simchah later explained: "Initially I saw that, due to his great fear, he was beyond help. After I joked with him, however, he became somewhat more cheerful and relaxed, and this enabled me to help save him from his plight" (*Midrash Simchah* 6).

The significant rôle which Simchah plays in personal growth and achievement can be seen clearly by observing a baby. One of the first voluntary expressions that a baby achieves is the ability to smile. The reason the Creator implanted the character trait of Simchah in man from such a young age is that an atmosphere of Simchah is essential to all development, both physical and spiritual.

Simchah —
The Secret of Success

Rav Chaim Vital (*Sha'arei Kedushah* 2:3) explains how melancholy stagnates spiritual growth:

> "Melancholy prevents one from serving G-d, performing mitzvot, studying Torah and concentrating during prayer. Furthermore, it also

obstructs the mere thought of serving G-d
from entering one's mind. It is the Evil Inclination's *initial step* towards causing man to
sin. Conversely, serving HaShem with Simchah causes a person to feel a great surge of
desire to become unified with G-d."

Since *the will* to serve G-d is the most important component of spiritual development, we can understand why Rav
Chaim Vital describes melancholy as the Evil Inclination's
initial stage of attack against a person's soul. When a person feels depressed, his will begins to crumble. Consequently, his ability to serve HaShem is greatly impaired.

The Sabah of Kelm *(Chachmah U'mussar* II p. 172) beauti-
fully describes this concept: "In comparison to deeds which
are performed with a strong will, deeds performed without
any will are like an effect without a cause. One should
ponder this thought and consider what spiritual heights a
person could reach were he to perform all his actions with
zeal. For zeal increases one's strength, elevates his
thoughts, and precludes indolence. A person's soul will
yearn to walk the path of wisdom and spiritual achievement. It is for this reason that the Torah is so stringent
about the Jewish People's lack of Simchah: Lack of Simchah
is, in reality, a lack of feeling and zeal, for they are in essence one. The stronger the will a person has, the more
successful he will be."

Indeed, Simchah is the spark of life — *the* spark which
ignites our ambition to rise to the heights of self-fulfillment
and success. It is the driving force behind all human development from the very start of life.

2

DEPRESSION

Just as it is a mitzvah to feel Simchah, it is prohibited to feel despondent. The Rambam writes (Commentary on *Mishnayot, Berachot*): "The warnings against feeling unhappiness and worry are so explicitly written in the books of the Prophets that there is no need to even talk about the subject". Alternatively, the *Me'or VaShemesh* (*Parshat BeH'alotchah*) explains that the source of this prohibition is the *Zohar*, which states that sadness has elements of idolatry. Similarly, *Sefer Toldot Ya'akov Yosef* (*Parshat VeEtchanan*) writes: "Worry and melancholy are the root of all evil." Rabbi Yabe (Psalms 6) explains that since the *Shechinah* (the Holy presence) does not dwell in a place of sadness, an individual who feels in low spirits is effectively abandoned by G-d. As a result, he is left without any protection to guard him against the Evil Inclination.

Unhappiness affects a person in the opposite manner than does Simchah. As opposed to Simchah, which nurtures the will to realize one's potential, despondency stunts one's will to grow and develop. The Vilna Gaon writes (Proverbs 15:13): "Feeling sad breaks a person's will. One whose will is broken will not achieve anything at all."

What Causes Unhappiness

Failure to achieve one's goals in life is the predominant cause of sadness. According to the Ralbag, this is the intention of the verse (Proverbs 13:12), "Expectation long deferred makes the heart sick; but a desire which is fulfilled is a tree of life." That is, the failure to achieve a long - sought - after goal makes the heart sick.

The Vilna Gaon (*Aderet Eliyahu, Bereshit* 1:3) infers this principle from the Sages' statement, "Every place where the word 'And it was (ויהי)' occurs, connotes forthcoming calamity."

The Vilna Gaon explains: "The word 'it will be (יהי)' is in the future tense. When it is prefixed by the letter *vav*, however, its meaning changes to 'and it *was*', which is in the past tense. The explanation for this grammatical transition is based on the fact that it is irrational to feel disappointment for failing to achieve something which is beyond one's capabilities. It is only reasonable for a person to feel disappointment when he fails to achieve goals that are *within* his capabilities. Thus, the word ויהי connotes the disappointment felt by someone who fails to realize his full potential. It indicates that when achievements which were within one's potential — יהי, pass one by and recede into the past — ויהי, one's world [his expected future] has been turned upside down."

The Effects of Sadness

Sadness causes a person to think that something which he desires is not within his grasp. Once he loses faith in himself and suffers one defeat after another, he begins to take refuge behind thoughts such as, "What difference does anything make anyhow? Everything is lost!" Consequently, *this thought breaks his internal will*. He loses hope of ever achieving the goal he seeks, which, in turn, prevents him from making further efforts in this direction. This is one of the methods which the Evil Inclination implements in order to prevent an individual's spiritual development. Concerning melancholy, Rabbi Yisrael Salanter wrote (*Or Yisrael* 7): "There is no greater disease than the loss of hope." This trait is the root of all spiritual atrophy. Rabbi Aharon of Karlin said: "Although feeling sadness is not explicitly prohibited by the Torah, even the most serious transgressions which *are* explicitly prohibited do not distort a person's perception of reality as does melancholy. It leads one to the very depths of Hell."

The Talmud (*Berachot* 52a) says: "Rav said: 'A sigh breaks half a man's body.' Rav Yochanan said 'It breaks the entire body.' " This illustrates the extent of the destructive power of melancholy. It is more harmful to the body than actual blows, as the Talmud (*Berachot* 55a) says: "A bad dream causes more discomfort than a public lashing."

Overcoming Melancholy

As we have established above, sadness is the result of feeling that one's goals are *totally beyond one's grasp*. Therefore, common sense dictates that there are two methods by which to overcome sadness: First, by changing one's attitude, so that one comes to realize that one's goals *are* within one's grasp. Second, in some instances, by realistically limiting one's expectations. Let's discuss this last method first.

Limiting One's Expectations

People sometimes fall into depression because they make unrealistic demands of themselves. Someone who expects too much of himself will invariably encounter failure. In turn, this experience will cause him to lose faith in himself, plunging him even further into a state of depression. Eventually, the snowballing lack of self-confidence will prevent him from achieving those goals which *were* well within his capabilities.

In order to break out of depression, a person must make a realistic reassessment of his or her capabilities. Introspection and the consequent conclusions will contribute a great deal toward overcoming melancholy.

Furthermore, many goals that people aspire to are not actually in their best interests. Only HaShem knows what is truly beneficial in the long run. Therefore, the wise person qualifies his aspirations. He desires their fulfillment only on the condition that they conform to the Will of HaShem — whatever that might be. This person will not be disappointed if his specific goals are not fulfilled, because he realizes that the mercy of HaShem's heavenly wisdom did not deem those goals to be the best for him. (These ideas have been discussed at length at the end of Part 1.)

The Second Method: Realizing the Falseness of Despair

The overriding feeling in a state of depression is despair. In most cases, this feeling is a result of one's imagination, which the Evil Inclination uses to exaggerate the importance of whatever obstacles caused the despair. Thus, a person should take care not to fall prey to this trap. When he experiences a defeat, the immediate emotional reaction is often one of despair. Instead, one must not lose hope, but exert oneself to distinguish between emotion and fact, and try to gather the strength to overcome the present situation. After "sleeping it over," one frequently realizes that he sees things in a different light, and the problem or obstacle may not be so serious after all. The negative emotion of despair is one of the most deadly weapons employed by the Evil Inclination.

The Sin of the Spies' Report

The spies sent out by Moses to investigate the Land of Canaan (Eretz Yisrael) reported (*Bamidbar* 14:1) that Eretz Yisrael was inhabited by *nefillim* — commonly translated as "giants", but literally, "those that cause others to fall". Supposedly, these people made everyone who saw them tremble with fright and just hearing about them caused the entire Jewish People *to cry*. When HaShem heard this, He decreed that both the First and Second Temples should be destroyed. In addition, the entire adult population was sentenced to die in the desert, rather than enter the Holy Land. Let us analyze the nature of this sin.

Although it is evident that before the spies' report, the great challenge of conquering Eretz Yisrael weighed heavily on the Jewish People's hearts. Still, they did not consider the task impossible. Furthermore, if, in spite of the spies' report, they had strengthened their awareness and faith that everything is within HaShem's power, and that He would somehow bring them into Eretz Yisrael, they would have succeeded in overcoming all the obstacles. Instead, the act of crying after hearing the spies' report revealed their lack of faith in HaShem and their loss of hope. Then it was no longer feasible for them to have any confidence in their ability to succeed. Subsequently this attitude caused their will to enter Israel to wither, and this was the primary cause for their not being allowed to enter Eretz Yisrael.

Thus, it is evident that the sin resulting from the spies' report was due to the Jewish People's absolute loss of hope — the *nefeillah*, the falling, which manifested itself through their tears. This unfortunate episode in Jewish history was only the first of many encounters through the generations, in which the Evil Inclination successfully wielded the deadly weapon of despair against the Jewish People.

What lesson should we learn from the Torah's account of the spies' report? It is as follows: The Jewish People felt that their situation was absolutely hopeless and that it was not within their power to overcome the obstacles before them. However, we see that eventually HaShem *did* enable them to vanquish nation after nation. As it turned out, when the Jewish People were poised outside Eretz Yisrael, it was these very nations dwelling in the Land who actually sat trembling, awaiting their imminent destruction. As the verse says (Joshua 2:11): "When we heard this, our hearts melted, and no more courage remained in any man, because of you. For the Lord your G-d alone is G-d, in the heavens above and on the earth below."

This is a perfect example that the willingness to give up is often based on falsehood and deception, which is one of the Evil Inclination's methods employed to destroy us. It impedes one from gathering his strength to overcome the actual obstacles, and instead his will decreases, until eventually he surrenders.

In contrast, the continuation of the story of our Nation's conquering the Land, demonstrates the result of never losing hope. Although the Jewish People faced apparently insurmountable odds, their unshakable belief in G-d and in their leader, Yehoshua, enabled them to vanquish their enemies. This, then, is how we may rectify the sin of the spies' report: by maintaining an unshakable conviction that no matter how difficult the challenges we face may seem, with G-d's help, we can and *will* succeed in strengthening our desire to come closer to Him.

3

DO NOT DESPAIR

The Danger in Falling

A person who struggles to achieve his goal but does not succeed, can become overwhelmed by a sense of deep despair and hopelessness. The oppressiveness of his situation seems to hinder all his efforts to regain his self-esteem and leads to further desperation and despondency.

Reb Chaim Shmulevitz, Ztz"l, brings an example of such a sudden downfall resulting from the psychological shock of failure (*Sichot Mussar* Yr. 5731, *Ma'amar* 13):

> "Orpah, the daughter-in-law of Naomi, was at first equal to Ruth in her desire to adhere to the G-d of Israel, as we read: 'And [Ruth and Orpah] said to [Naomi], 'We shall return with you to your people.' Naomi said, 'Return, my daughters....' They raised their voices and wept even more. Then Orpah kissed her mother-in-law farewell, but Ruth clung to her' (Ruth 1:10-14). At first, both Ruth and Orpah spoke the same words and

pleaded the same plea. Orpah had arrived at the same conviction as Ruth, to the extent of being ready to leave her own people and homeland and to live as a convert in Israel. However, after Naomi told them to go back, she could not withstand the trial and decided to depart. Ruth, in contrast, clung to her mother-in-law and ascended to lofty spiritual heights. (We will discuss this episode in greater detail below.) Orpah did not have that strength, she entirely lost her drive to become a Jewess and returned to her old way of life. Her spiritual fall was so great, that Chazal (*Ruth Rabbah*, 2) relate: "On that same night that Orpah had departed from her mother-in-law, she prostituted herself with an army unit of a hundred men....Rav Tanchuma says, 'Also one dog.' "

The story of Ruth and Orpah can serve to strengthen us through many challenges in life. We are constantly in the midst of two polarized situations — either a state of ascent, or a state of descent. When a person perceives that he is descending, he must intensify his efforts to strengthen himself, so that he does not continue to fall.

The method to overcome melancholy during a period of descent is described by HaRav HaKadosh, Reb Aharon of Karlin, Ztz"l (*Sefer Beit Aharon*): "And if, G-d forbid, he shall fall prey to the Evil Inclination, [that is to say, that he was unsuccessful in performing the mitzvah properly], he should not become melancholic as a result, for melancholy causes a person to fall into evil habits, G-d forbid. Instead, he *should forget about it* and make every effort to improve in the future."

Rejected — But Not Fallen

The Fallen of Beitar

We learn in the *Gemara* (*Berachot* 48b):

> "Rav Masna said, 'On the day when the fallen
> of Beitar were handed over for burial, in
> Yavneh they instituted the benediction *HaTov
> VeHaMetiv*: *HaTov* (He who is good), because
> they did not smell bad, and *HaMetiv* (He who
> does good), because they were allowed to be
> buried."

Beitar constituted the last spark of hope for the Jewish People's spiritual redemption. Its fall caused total spiritual darkness to descend. Yet the Sages of Yavneh considered the burial of the Beitar victims as a kindness which was greater than all others, a sign that even when Darkness was allowed to rule in the world, Divine Providence was still with them.

This is a lesson for us, too. Even if the Almighty has allowed us to become degraded to a certain extent, He does not wish our downfall. Rather, if we know what to look for, we find constant reminders that He continues to show us love and sympathy in times of distress. We should never despair or give up hope.

Overcoming Despair

We learn in the Torah (*Devarim* 20:1):

> "When you go out to make war on your foes
> and you see horses and chariots, people who

outnumber you — do not fear them, for
HaShem, your G-d, is with you, Who brought
you up from the land of Egypt."

Furthermore, the High Priest appointed for the war is
commanded to strengthen the hearts of the warriors, en-
couraging them in order that their spirits do not fall. The
Torah even released from duty those who feared the war,
so that the remaining soldiers would not be influenced by
their fear (ibid. 20:8). The passage ends with the verse:
"When the guards finish commanding the people, they
shall appoint officers to head the people." Rashi explains
that "guards are stationed before them and behind them
with iron bars in their hands. Whoever attempts to escape,
they are authorized to beat him up. Guards: people who
stand upright, whose task it is to raise the spirits of those
whose spirits are low, and to tell them, 'Return to the bat-
tlefield and do not flee, for fleeing is the beginning of defeat.' "

In these Torah verses, the Jewish Nation is commanded
to overcome despair in time of war. However, this also
represents the correct approach to our personal wars. The
Torah commands: "Fear them not!"

King David said (Psalm 27:14): "Hope to HaShem, be
strong and your heart be of courage, and hope to
HaShem." The Yavetz comments: "This [imperative] applies to every person who is in trouble, that he should not
despair, but 'hope to HaShem'. If his wish does not come
true, his heart should be of courage and hope yet further
and his wish will not be turned down."

The Spiritual Endurance of Israel's Kings

One of the most essential traits of a king is the will to overcome obstacles under all circumstances, and never surrender to an enemy. The kings of Israel are shining examples of individuals who personify this trait.

Ruth

Let us start with the ancestor of Israel's dynasty of kings, Ruth the Moabitess.

We read in the Book of Ruth (1:1-3): "Now it came to pass in the days when the Judges ruled, that there was a famine in the land. Elimelech of Beitlechem-Yehudah, went to sojourn in the country of Moab. He, Elimelech, and his wife, Naomi, and his two sons..." Elimelech, Naomi's husband, died, and she remained with her two sons.

In the Malbim's commentary, he explains that Elimelech was one of the prominent leaders of the Jewish People in that generation. Although one of the obligations of a leader is to give encouragement to his people during difficult times, Elimelech was found lacking in this respect. When a terrible famine came upon Eretz Yisrael, he abandoned his people and fled to Moab, leaving them without a leader to guide them. As one can imagine, this made their spirits sink even further, and the Sages say he was punished with death for this act.

"And they [Machlon and Chilyon, Elimelech's two sons] took wives for themselves of the women of Moab. The name of one was Orpah and the name of the other, Ruth. They dwelt there about ten years." Ruth was the daughter of Eglon, King of Moab. She grew up as a princess in the royal house and married the son of Elimelech, one of the most prominent families of Israel.

Her days of serenity did not last, however, and her situation deteriorated from bad to worse. Chazal say (quoted in Rashi, ibid., 1:8): "At first they were punished economically, and their livestock died. Later they [Machlon and Chilyon, Ruth and Orpa's husbands] died too."

In spite of her tremendous fall from the status of a princess, daughter of the king, to a poor, hungry widow, Ruth nonetheless clung to her mother-in-law, Naomi: "So Naomi went forth out of the place where she was, her two daughters-in-law with her. They went on the way, to return to the land of Judah."

In spite of all the good will that Ruth had demonstrated, Naomi explained to her daughter-in-law that there was no sense continuing on with her to Judah, as there seemed to be no hope of finding a better life there. Orpah was discouraged and gave up her desire to follow Naomi, as we discussed above. Orpah's retreat however did not affect Ruth's strong will and courage: "But Ruth clung to her." Ruth's great emotional strength in refusing to despair in any situation, and her determination to be part of the Jewish nation, eventually led to the birth of the father of royalty: "Boaz begot Obed, and Obed begot Yishai, and Yishai begot David."

David

David, the first king from the royal tribe of Yehuda, inherited this strength of character from his great-grandmother Ruth.

We learn in the first Book of Samuel (I 17:4-32): "A champion went forth out of the Philistine encampment; Goliath was his name, of Gat. His height [was] six cubits and a span. [He had] a helmet of brass on his head and he was wearing a shield-coat of scales. The weight of the shield-coat [was] five thousand *shekalim* brass....When Saul and all Israel heard those words of the Philistine, they were dismayed and very afraid.... David said to [the King], 'Let no man's heart fall because of him; your servant will go and fight with this Philistine."

We are impressed with David's courage and refusal to despair as he volunteered to fight against Goliath.

This character trait helped David rule over the Jewish nation and lead the armies of Isreal against all the powerful enemies that rose against him. It also helped him overcome all the difficult episodes in his personal life. An example of King David's courageous attitude, whatever the situation, is when he was forced to flee from his son Avshalom, who had rebelled against him (Samuel II 15:30): "David went up by the ascent of [Mount] Olives, weeping as he went. His head was covered, and he was barefoot." At that solemn moment, David was informed that his faithful advisor Achitofel had joined the rebels (ibid., 15:31). Even at that time of deep distress, David did not fall into despair, but prayed to HaShem, confident of His ultimate salvation: 'David said, 'HaShem, I pray to You, turn the counsel of Achitofel into foolishness.' " Not only did David not despair; on the contrary, he began to sing (Psalms 3:1): "A psalm of David when he fled from Avshalom his son...."

The Talmud (*Berachot* 7b) further explains that David was even able to see something positive in the situation: He was glad that the rebel was his son and not a slave, for had that been the case, his situation would have been far worse. The conspirators would have certainly handled him with cruelty and brutality.

Solomon

Solomon, David's son continued the chain of royalty exhibiting strength and courage during the hardest of times.

King Solomon reigned over the entire world, over all the creatures, even the demons (*Gittin* 68a). In the and, however, he was dethroned and deposed of his greatness, and he "reigned only over his wooden staff" (*Sanhedrin* 20b). HaGaon Reb Chaim Shmulevitch, Ztz"l, explains (*Sichot U'Mussar*, Yr. 5731, p.43): "The wisest of all men deployed tricks in order that he would not fall into despair and gloom, G-d forbid. What did he do? He *remained* king — over his staff!"

What exactly did our Sages mean when they said that "he ruled over his staff"? How can there be royal government over a wooden staff?

The matter may be explained in this way: The royalty of Israel is authentic and eternal, not superficial and temporary. The main characteristic of a Jewish leader is his ability to rule over *himself*, his desires and his temptations. In the Midrash (*Bereshit Rabbah* 99) we learn: "The Creator said [to Yehuda], 'You admitted your deed concerning Tamar, therefore your brothers shall acknowledge your kingdom over them.' " In other words, *because* he had the courage to be king over himself, admitting his guilt, he shall become the future King over Israel.

The kingdom of Solomon, too, was a kingdom of truth, based on the rule of a man who succeeded in controlling himself. The Prophet tells us (I Kings 5:9): "HaShem gave wisdom to Solomon... like the sand which is on the shore of the sea." The Midrash explains (*Yalkut* II 177): "Rav Levi said, 'Like the sand is a barrier to the sea, so was the wisdom of Solomon a barrier for him....' " Solomon ruled over himself through his wisdom. It was a barrier to his spirit and tamed his emotions and his body. This, apparently, is what Chazal meant by the expression that he "ruled over his staff," symbolizing the power of overcoming his Evil Inclination.

Although Solomon was deposed of his royal government and no longer reigned over the world, he still remained King Solomon. His spirit did not fall, because he had a great sense of satisfaction from his reign *over himself*, just as if he reigned over the entire world.

The Leaders of the Jewish Nation

Although we no longer have kings to rule over us, nevertheless, we merit in their stead — the Rabbis and Sages of every generation, as the Talmud says: "Who is a king? The Sages." The following is only one of countless anecdotes which illustrate the Sages' strength of will, courage and perseverance.

The Gaon, Reb Chaim Shmulevitz, Ztz"l, the former Head of the great Mir Yeshivah, taught Torah and strengthened the faith of his students under the most horrifying and difficult conditions, when the Yeshiva was exiled to Japan during World War II. The Japanese prohibited anyone who did not live in the Jewish ghetto to remain there after nightfall, and residents could only leave the ghetto with special permission.

One night, the Japanese Secret Service made a surprise visit to Reb Chaim's home. Reb Chaim and his study partner, who lived outside the ghetto, were arrested. It was feared that a thorough search of the house would soon follow. The search would have revealed a large sum of American dollars, which Reb Chaim kept in his hope to sustain the Yeshivah. This discovery could have had very serious consequences, since Japanese law forbade the possession of American currency.

Death hovered over Reb Chaim's head, and the situation appeared desperate. Reb Chaim, however, did not allow this predicament to break his spirit or affect his service of G-d. He spent the remainder of the night reviewing a certain section of Tractate *Shabbat*, and then a miracle occurred....For some unknown reason, the Secret Service failed to carry out the dreaded search until much later, and in the meantime word was sent to Reb Chaim's wife to take the dollars out of the house (*Moach VeLev*, Chapter 6).

Reb Chaim's extraordinary ability to remain calm during this frightening experience stemmed from his ability not to fall into despair, but to serve HaShem under all circumstances.

Who could tell of all the countless demonstrations of strength of character which the great Sages of every generation possessed? They were the navigators who led the Jewish People to safe shores during the most tempestuous times. They stood by to give support to those who fell into despair throughout our extended Exile. Yet *every* Jew is akin to a prince. We all have ingrained within ourselves the essential traits of royalty. If we will only try, we will discover the exceptional strength of character necessary to overcome *all* obstacles!

4

CONFUSION

We have seen above that there is a direct relationship between man's will to fulfill his potential and whether or not he feels Simchah. The most essential component in reinforcing one's will is to make a firm decision to reach one's goal. The relationship between happiness and resolution is implied in the Hebrew word for cry — בכיה — which stems from the word מבוכה, "confusion". It says in the verse (*Shemot* 14:3): "Pharaoh will say of the children of Israel, 'They are entangled [נבוכים] in the land, the wilderness has shut them in.' " The act of crying indicates a person's confusion about the future, which, in turn, causes him to fall into despair. On the other hand, one who feels secure about the direction he has taken, feels content and happy, for he sees his path clearly in front of him. This feeling of contentment gives him the strength necessary to achieve his goals.

The *Akedat Yitzchak* (98) describes this state of mind as follows: "One should not agree to do things which he is not certain are worthwhile, for anyone who feels uncertain about the worth of his deeds will invariably perform his tasks with reluctance and indolence. This is proven from the account of Yoav ben Tzruyah, who was commanded by King David to take a census of the Jewish People. Because he did not understand the reason for the census, as the verse (Shmuel II 24:3) says, 'Why does my master the King wish this thing?', he was found at fault for three reasons: First, he initially refused to comply with King David's command. Second, he did not complete the assignment, for he failed to count the tribes of Levy and Binyamin, as the verse says: (Chronicles I 21:6) 'He did not include Levy and Binyamin in the census, for Yoav detested the order of the King.' Third, he failed to ascertain the exact number of people he counted."

In contrast, when a person feels content with the task he has been assigned, he is able to perform it swiftly and efficiently, as the verse testifies (*Bereshit* 29:1): "Ya'akov lifted his legs and he went to the land of Benei Kedem." Rashi explains the meaning of the words "lifted his legs": "The moment Ya'akov was assured a safe journey, his heart was lightened and it became easy to walk."

The following Midrash also illustrates this concept (*Vayikrah Rabbah* 34:8):

> "Rav Yitzchak said: 'Scripture teaches us that if one is to perform a task, he should do it *with a cheerful heart*, for had Reuven known that Hashem would later write in the Torah the verse 'Reuven heard, and he saved him from their hands,' he would have carried him (Yosef) on his shoulders. Had Aharon known that Hashem would later write in the Torah 'See, he [Aharon] is coming out to greet you,' he would have come out to greet him with

musical instruments and dancers. Had Boaz
known that Hashem would later write [in the
Book of Ruth] the verse 'And he gave her
[Ruth] roasted grains, and she ate and was
satisfied, and there was even left over,' he
would have fed her fattened calves."

On the above, the *Tifferet Tzion* (Ruth Rabah 5:6) raises an
obvious difficulty: Is it reasonable to consider that righteous people such as Reuven, Aharon, and Boaz would
have allowed the knowledge that their actions would eventually be recorded in Scripture to influence them? Even
without the consideration of an eternal record of their actions, wasn't their every thought and action intended to
comply with the divine Will of G-d?

In accordance with the principles we have discussed, we
could answer as follows: Reuven, Aharon, and Boaz were
unsure that their actions were correct. Reuven's hesitation
stemmed from his concern that perhaps his brothers' judgment was right, that Yosef in fact deserved the death pen-
alty. Similarly, Aharon was reluctant to accept Moshe's
appointment as leader of Israel, out of concern that this
position should be awarded to him as the elder brother
[legally, not because of any desire for personal power or
prestige]. Boaz, too, was concerned about the propriety of
offering Ruth food, since this act could comprise a legally
binding act of marriage. In addition, he feared that offering
her food would be an immodest act. These doubts are what
prevented Reuven, Aharon and Boaz from behaving in the
manner described by the Midrash; *uncertainty* effectively
disrupted their ability to perform each action wholeheartedly. Had they been certain that their actions were in accordance with the Divine Will, it would have strengthened

their resolve and enabled them to have acted unhindered by the weight of indecision.

We learn a valuable lesson from this Midrash: Indecision, lack of direction and low self-esteem invariably lead to dejection and a state of depression, which, in turn, brings emotional collapse and failure in its wake. The Midrash exhorts us to "Perform a task...with a cheerful heart," which, as we have seen, requires one to resolve whatever doubts occupy one's mind.

Similarly, casting doubts in people's minds was the basic weapon employed by Amalek against the Jewish People in the desert. Prior to their attack against the Jews, the nations of the world feared the consequences of attacking the Jewish People.

They were afraid that the same fate which befell the Egyptians would occur to them. By attacking the Jewish People, Amalek effectively caused the other nations to question their fear of the Jews. They demonstrated that the Jews were as vulnerable as any other nation, and that anyone who wished to attack them need not fear Heavenly Retribution.

This quality is in fact the very essence of Amalek, as is evident from the *gematria* of that name: the Hebrew letters of "Amalek" (עמלק) have the same numerical value as those of the Hebrew word for "doubt"(ספק)! Thus, we must recognize that there exist spiritual forces whose primary goal is to cast doubt in people's minds, in order to hinder their spiritual growth.

Overcautiousness

From the teachings of HaRav HaKadosh, Reb Asher of Stollin Ztz"l (quoted in *Sefer Beit Aharon* p. 3), we learn: "A person must be aware of the great danger which lies in developing an exaggerated sense of scrupulousness as one of his guidelines in the observance and performance of all his actions. Very often this creates feelings of insecurity, fear and sadness that essential obligations and responsibilities are not being fulfilled properly. Thus, playing directly into the hands of the *yetzer hora*, whose sole purpose is to divert us and diminish our connection to Torah. Insecurity, fear and sadness are major hindrances in the service of HaShem."

In Halachah, scrupulousness must indeed be observed without any leniency. However, one should avoid imposing upon himself additional, noncompulsory stringencies which are beyond his ability. In the words of the *Chovot HaLevavot* (Preface): "Caution also includes the lack of exaggeration when being cautious," because an overstated sense of strictness might lead to heresy, G-d forbid. If a person cannot follow through, he might avoid doing the mitzvah altogether. HaGaon Rav Yisroel Kanievsky expresses the same thought in several letters, (quoted in *Eitzot VeHadrachot* p.102. We also find the same concept in *Sefer HaYosher*, Chapter 6).

The most common time for such doubts to occur is during the performance of important mitzvot, such as when sitting down to study Torah. Suddenly we find ourselves wondering whether we should be fulfilling some other mitzvah at this time. Yet this is exactly the moment when we must remind ourselves that this is another attempt by the Evil Inclination to disrupt our ability to serve G-d. One should simply ignore the doubts which enter one's mind, and remember that "One involved in a mitzvah is free from performing other mitzvot" (*Succah* 25a).

How to Remove Oneself from Confusion

Since confusion is a major obstacle to achieving Simchah, one should constantly strive to be confident about everything that he or she does. This is true concerning mitzvot as well as noncompulsory deeds, as we shall explain further.

To acquire such confidence, there are several conditions:

A) One should pray to HaShem to open one's eyes and mind to be receptive to the way of truth.

B) One should try to gain and maintain a clear picture of the various options and utilize the great gift given one by the Creator — one's mind — to decide which is the best path to follow in each specific situation.

C) At times, the person directly involved does not possess sufficient peace of mind to evaluate the situation correctly. When this is the case, a wise friend who also knows how to listen should be consulted.

D) When the matter requires professional advice, an expert in the field should be consulted. At times it is necessary to consult an expert in worldly matters, and at times consultation with a *Posek* or a Rav is required.

E) When a rabbi is consulted, his ruling must be accepted. There is no room for doubt as to whether or not he is properly equipped to make the correct decision. As we learn (*Devorim* 17:9): "You shall come to the *Kohanim*, the

Levites and to the judges that will be in those days." Chazal comment (*Rosh HaShanah* 25a): "You should go only to the judge of your own time."

One should consult a Torah scholar on a regular basis (not just in the midst of a crisis) and follow his advice and instructions concerning all aspects of life. In this way, through his wisdom and objectivity, we avoid confusion. As Rabban Gamliel said (*Avot* 1:16): "Acquire for yourself a rabbi, and avoid doubts."

F) Upon receiving the proper advice, one must strictly adhere to it and resolve that this is the path to travel, since he has fulfilled every obligation to discern the truth.

When a person acts in accordance with what he has resolved to do, he should do it with Simchah and without hesitation. This is the meaning of the verse (Chronicles II 17:6): "His heart was lifted in the ways of HaShem" — One should feel honored when walking in the ways of HaShem and not give in to temptations from without, and doubts from within, that cloud the mind.

Worldly Actions

This attitude applies not only to the performance of actual mitzvot, but also with regard to any worldly actions that are essential for a person or for the benefit of the world. They, too, are considered mitzvot, and it is the Will of HaShem that a person should also occupy himself with the material world in which He placed us. As we learn (*Bereshit* 1:28): "HaShem blessed them and He told them, 'Be fruitful and multiply, fill the world and conquer it....Look, I have given thee all the grass that makes seed that is on the face of the earth.' " (This idea is expressed in *Chovot HaLevavot, Avodat HaShem,* Chapter 4.) Since all of a person's actions fall within the category of either mitzvot or sins, he should perform those deeds that *are* the Will of HaShem — whether spiritual or material — with Simchah, confidence and assurance, without any doubt or hesitation.

Ignoring Confusion over One's Decisions

There are two kinds of confusion:

A) *Intellectual perplexity* (confusion of the mind), regarding matters which are permissible, possible and even obligatory to search and investigate.

B) *Emotional perplexity* (confusion of the heart), concerning matters that a person may not be sufficiently equipped to deal with from an emotional standpoint. For example, a *ba'al t'shuvah* at times feels an emotional clash between the way of life to which he was accustomed, and the new Torah way of life. Although this person is fully and intellectually aware that this is the true path that he should follow, he is emotionally perplexed, nonetheless.

The way to avoid intellectual confusion of the first category is to clarify the matter thoroughly (as explained above). On the other hand, the way to circumvent the perplexity of the second kind of doubts, those which result from feelings that overwhelm the mind, is to *ignore* the perturbing thoughts.

The Sabbah of Kelm wrote (*Kitvei Sabbah* 23): "There is an important rule: If one has a conviction and has already made up his mind, then [he will find that] the *will power* to ignore any doubt which creeps in is stronger than any advice in the world." The reason this technique works is that a face-to-face battle is likely to intensify this type of doubt and to increase the perplexity. In the words of Reb Yisroel Salanter (printed in *Ohr HaMussar*, Vol. 10, 586): "[The right way is] not through exerting a concentrated effort to counter the [troubling] thoughts, for the way of human nature is that the more one tries to suppress a certain [emotion producing] thought, the more strongly it will rise to the surface. Therefore, excessive efforts to suppress the thoughts might at times produce the opposite results of those desired."

We see, then, that after one has diffused the thoughts and doubts that stem from the emotions, in an intellectual manner, and even tried to get them "out of his system" by discussing them with a close friend, one should then *ignore them* and continue on his way, with Simchah. It's all a matter of time; the more a person gets used to the new situation and adheres to the way he knows is right, the more confident and content he will be.

Dealing with the "Negative Aspect"

There are times when a person plunges into confusion as a result of something negative in a particular situation. For example, he purchased something that has a defect, or he finds himself with a study partner who is not appropriate for him, or he works at a job that is not to his liking. The negative aspect creates doubts as to the value of his actions and he may begin to think that whatever he is doing is a mistake or without purpose. One must strengthen himself, that if he has indeed resolved that this is the thing to do, all these doubts are nothing more than subversive messages of the *yetzer hora*. Instead, he should ascend to a higher level and consider the positive aspects of his actions. In this way, he will regain his sense of purpose and be satisfied with his accomplishments.

Avraham Avinu

Our forefather Avraham exemplifies the ability to rise above doubt and continue to serve G-d with intense devotion. The verse (*Bereshit* 22:20) says:

"*After these things,* G-d said to Avraham, 'Behold, Milkah too has borne children to Nachor your brother.' "

Rashi writes: "When Avraham returned from Mount Moriah [where G-d had commanded him to sacrifice Yitzchak], he thought to himself, 'Had my son been slaughtered, he would have left this world without having children. I should have married him to one of the daughters of Enner, Eshkol or Mamreh.' "

One may wonder why Avraham did not consider this thought *before* arriving at Mount Moriah, since he knew then that Yitzchak's death was imminent. The answer is that Avraham did not want to mar the fulfillment of a commandment [to sacrifice Yitzchak] by fostering doubt in his heart as to whether or not he should have married off his son long ago. Instead, he held his doubts at bay until *after* the completion of the mitzvah.

Avraham's ability to overcome his doubts and persist in the service of G-d is eternal proof that it is indeed possible to screen our thoughts and emotions, to be selective as to which thoughts we allow to influence our consciousness.

After all, Avraham was a man who questioned every given, who had the nature and strength to challenge his entire generation's idolatrous beliefs single-handedly. And yet, he was able to overcome his skeptical nature, to hold off his doubting in the face of the Almighty's Will.

How much more, then, should we be able to ignore our inner skepticism and to let ourselves go in the direction we know to be right. This degree of self-control is certainly within our reach.

Encouragement

Now that we understand the destructive force of confusion, we can appreciate the importance of encouragement. It is a "tool" which enables a person to ascend from the depths of perplexity, to gain strength and confidence that his is the right way.

We learn in the *Gemara* (*Sotah* 47a): "One should always reject with the left hand and bring close with the right hand...unlike Elisha, who pushed Gehazi with both hands." How destructive is the power of rejection: it can break a friend's spirit and totally deter him from the right path. On the other hand, how great is encouragement from a friend — it uplifts one's spirit and gives him or her the strength to cope with difficult situations, to ascend and grow.

Sometimes a person makes a decision or closes a deal, and then turns to his friend for an opinion. At this point, the friend must remember that there is no way to turn back the clock, and instead, it is his duty to do all he can in order to make his friend happy, to cheer him up with words and avoid making any negative comments about the matter.

We find this principle in the words of our Sages (*Ketubot* 17a):

> "How does one dance before the bride? Beit Shammai says, '[Praise the] bride according to her actual beauty,' and Beit Hillel says, 'Beautiful and gracious bride.' Beit Shammai said to Beit Hillel, 'Suppose she is a cripple or blind — [would you] say beautiful and gracious bride? The Torah commands: You shall keep away from a word of lie.' Beit Hillel said to Beit Shammai, 'According to your opinion, if a person made a poor deal in the market, should [his friend] praise it or should he criticize it? Surely he should praise it. From this our Rabbis learn: One should always be pleasant to people.' "

The Tosfot explain that Beit Shammai concedes to Beit Hillel, and that one should praise his friend's purchase even if the deal was a bad one. Still, one should not say "beautiful and gracious bride," however, because our Sages would not instruct us to tell an outright lie. In any case, they decided the law according to Beit Hillel, demonstrating the great value of encouragement, even if at times it must override "absolute" truth.

The moral lesson we learn from these words is that we must always try to encourage our friend and emphasize the positive aspects of his actions, so that he may overcome his doubts and hesitations and be happy with what he has already done. Even if one thinks differently, he should make an effort to understand his friend's convictions and to encourage him *in accordance with the opinion of his friend!*

This concept which we call encouragement is not limited to words which one speaks to another. A person can also encourage *himself* and boost his own spirits by evaluating anew his ways and deeds, and strengthening his determination to realize his wishes and aspirations.

Conclusion

We have learned that the essence and basis of Simchah is a matter of being relieved of doubts and confusion. An issue which was investigated and decided upon already has to be considered *closed*. One must be calm and confident with his decision and have faith in HaShem, for He leads all who put their trust in Him on the right path. By avoiding confusion, a person can be wholeheartedly directed to act in Simchah!

5

HELPING OTHERS FEEL SIMCHAH

The Obligation to Help

In light of what has been established, that Simchah is the root of all growth and success, we can now appreciate the importance of helping others feel Simchah.

The Vilna Gaon explicitly states in a letter to his family that it is a positive mitzvah to cause others to feel Simchah: "I have also requested from my mother that there should be Shalom between you. You should both cheer each other with good words, for this is a great mitzvah which every person is obligated to fulfill. One of the questions a person is asked on the Day of Judgment is 'Did you treat your fellow Jew with kindness?' Thus, it is evident that one must treat others with kindness, for the Torah obligates one to cause others to feel Simchah."

The Reward for Helping

The Talmud reveals the extent of the reward one receives for causing others to feel Simchah with the following account: "The Prophet Eliyahu revealed to Rabbi Berokah that two people in the marketplace had earned a portion in the World to Come. Rabbi Berokah approached them and asked them what they had done. They answered that they were jesters who made sad people feel happy."

In addition to the promise of a portion in the World to Come, one who makes others feel cheerful receives a reward in *this world* as well. Everyone knows that helping others causes a person to be well-liked by his acquaintances. Furthermore, eventually those individuals whom he helps will reciprocate in kind. The Vilna Gaon derives this idea from the verse (Proverbs 11:25): "A beneficent soul will be abundantly gratified; and he that refreshes others will also be refreshed himself." He writes (ibid.): "A person who blesses others, shows concern for their welfare and does not feel jealousy towards them, will accordingly cause them to feel cheerful. He will cause their bones to expand [according to the *Talmud*, a physical symptom of happiness], and consequently, he himself will feel joyous."

The Method for Helping

The way to make a sad person happy is by understanding what hurts him, to empathize with his pain. King Solomon said (Proverbs 12:25): "If there be care in the heart of man, let him suppress it and a good word will change it into joy." Concerning this verse, Rabbi Ami and Rabbi Yossi said (*Yumah* 75a): "One of them said: 'One should distract him from his thoughts,' and the other one said: 'He should speak out his thoughts to others.'" In truth, these two opinions are complementary, since it is impossible to distract a person who feels deep emotional pain all at once. Therefore, if one wants to give him encouragement, it is not correct to tell him, "Forget your sorrows and be happy!" Instead, it is necessary to first share his pain with him and to pay attention to what bothers him. Only afterwards is it possible to bring up other subjects in the hope of distracting him from his misery.

Summary of Part Two

We have learned that there is an equilibrium between Active Simchah and a man's will. A person who is "B'Simchah" has an uplifted will, the spark of all growth and accomplishment. On the other hand, depression stunts one's will and makes him totally inactive. It is essential that a person protect this life-giving spark from extinction, by not giving up hope even in the darkest predicament. We should continuously try to fan this spark by being confident in our ways, so that it will turn into a iluminating bonfire, fueling growth and success.

PART III

TORAH-TRUE SIMCHAH

Simchah in Mitzvot

1

SIMCHAH THROUGH GROWTH

As has been mentioned earlier, emotional depression hinders the possibility of self-development, while Simchah is a principal positive component of personal development. In this chapter we will be dealing with the converse of this statement, which is also true: growth produces Simchah, while constriction brings sadness.

Rav Moshe Schapiro explained in a Torah discourse, that this concept is derived from the word שמחה itself, which is a variant of the root צמח, meaning *growth*. (The letters צ and ש often interchange in Hebrew.) This concept is also evident in the *Talmud* (*Eruvin* 3b), where the term "a 'sad' *amah*" [a unit of measurement] means an exact measure of one *amah*, while "a 'happy' *amah*" means a "generous *amah*," slightly larger than one *amah*. From this we see that the Sages of the *Talmud* considered it a self-evident fact that sadness causes a person to withdraw within himself, while joy produces expansion beyond one's limits.

The Maharal writes (*Netivot Olam, Gemilut Hasadim*): "When there is Simchah, there is growth and expansion. The opposite situation is when one is in low spirits or feels anguish. One who feels Simchah is in a state of growth."

The Constriction of Sadness

The negative qualities of sadness which we have described above are apparent in the Hebrew word for "sadness" — עצבות. It stems from the two letter root עץ, or "tree," which itself is derived from the word עצם — literally, "the essence of a thing." That is, sadness is similar to a bare tree before it has given forth fruit and realized its hidden potential. This is the opposite of Simchah, and makes one withdraw inward, preventing him from manifesting his skills and realizing his potential.

This is undoubtedly the reason behind the *halachah* which states that, given the choice, it is better to pray inside a closed area rather than out in the open, as the *Shulchan Aruch* says (*Orech Chaim* 90:5): "When one is in a modest place, the fear of the King affects him, and consequently his heart is broken." Being in an enclosed place limits one's vision, which subconsciously evokes thoughts concerning one's inability to realize his will and desires. The realization that one's very existence is dependent on Hashem's Will penetrates the heart, transforming prayer into a sincere plea for mercy. In contrast, an open field of vision elicits thoughts of future plans and unfulfilled ambitions. Confidence and optimism fill one's heart, precluding the need to beseech Hashem for mercy.

Simchah, on the other hand, always implies breaking through boundaries and the release from confinement. Therefore, we often find Simchah in such a context: "When you shall *set out* in Simchah" (Isaiah 55:12); "Happy as they *go out*" (Shabbat Morning Prayers).

Fulfilling a Task or Mission

We have explained above that Simchah implies action and growth — *sameach* (happy) in the sense of *tzemach* (plant). When a person is in a state of growth, elevating his qualities from the potential to the practical, he is automatically happy. When a person's talents and abilities remain only in the sphere of potential, however, he is unhappy, because he remains confined within his own boundaries, unable to break forth and grow.

Thus, the more a person feels that he is implementing his talents and potential abilities by rising to specific challenges, projects, or mitzvot — for example, through learning Torah, doing *chessed*, or in his trade and occupation, the happier he feels.

The same is true for a specific task. A person feels satisfaction when he accomplishes his task successfully with diligence and efficiency. Without a task or mission, on the other hand, he feels empty and sad. People in the field of child education know well that if a child is sad, it is advisable to give him a specific task. In fulfilling his assigned task, the child begins to feel useful and effective, and he finds contentment. Similarly, anyone who sets a certain goal for himself is happy when that goal is reached, because Simchah is the result of continued completion and growth.

Some Practical Advice

To induce the feeling of self-accomplishment one might want to list tasks to be accomplished. After completing each task, one crosses it off the list. In this way a sense of fulfillment will be felt as the list gets shorter.

The Cause of Sadness — Lack of Growth

If happiness depends upon growth, then we may assume that when someone is sad, it is because he is not expressing certain talents and abilities from within himself. Furthermore, the greater the potential talents and the more capable the person is, the more dissatisfied and upset he feels when he fails to utilize these abilities.

The way to overcome this undesirable situation and to ascend to the state of Simchah is, first of all, to gain insight into one's inner-self, in order to discover the special qualities with which he is uniquely blessed. From there, he can then proceed to make full use of these potential talents.

Every individual is blessed with special talents, and the more he succeeds in developing them, the happier he or she will be. There are times when a person is involved with matters that are not exactly in accordance with his qualifications, due to social pressure and the like. In such a situation, one should have mercy — do *chessed* — upon himself. He should do his utmost to relieve the external pressures by occupying himself with more suitable activities. (We have discussed this point at length at the end of Part One.)

Progressing from Stagnation to Growth

Quite often, one does not recognize his own abilities and talents. Experts in psychology know well that the average person utilizes a mere ten percent of his mental faculties.

How, then, can a person discover and realize all the powers within himself? We find the answer to this question in the words of HaGaon Rav Chaim Shmulevitz, Ztz"l, (*Sichot Mussar* 1977, p. 15):

> "[Regarding the People of Israel who were requested to contribute to the building of the Tabernacle,] we read: 'They came, every man *whose heart* moved him' (*Shemot* 35:21). The Ramban explains: 'This is said about the Wise Men who did the work, because there was no one among them who learned those particular crafts from a teacher, none who [previously] trained his hands in these particular works at all. Instead, each found it within his nature to know how to do it, and his heart exalted in the ways of HaShem, to come to Moshe and tell him 'I shall do all that my master speaks.'
>
> Seeing this great task — 'to think thoughts, to work in silver and in gold, in brass and in stone masonry' — an amateur who had never had any training in this vocation would normally throw up his hands in despair, protesting, 'How can I accept upon myself something that I know nothing about?' [In this case, however,] those whose *heart* had moved them came before Moshe with strength and with confidence, proclaiming, 'We shall do all that our master speaks.' Without hesitation or doubts, they accepted upon themselves the execution of what was needed for the work of the Tabernacle. This is because 'their hearts exalted in the ways of HaShem.' For there is no limit nor maximum as to what a self-respecting and practical person can achieve. With perfect confidence, he declares, 'I shall

do all that is necessary,' and thus, he really can do so.

This is also true regarding *B'nei Torah*. The one who says, 'Who am I and what am I, what can I achieve and how far can I reach?' will hesitate to try and will give up in despair. He did not reach the degree of 'his heart exalted in the ways of HaShem.' The self-respecting person knows that there is no limit to what he can achieve, and his heart exalts in the ways of HaShem to say, 'I shall reach the highest levels.' In this way, he *is* successful."

From here we gain a meaningful insight as to how we can transform a state of stagnation into one of growth. If we have a sense of self-respect and "exalt our hearts in the ways of HaShem," accepting tasks even though they may seem beyond our abilities. One's inner powers will then be revealed and blossom and bear fruit!

For example: Someone who is talented in a specific area of knowledge should foster a sense of pride for that ability with which HaShem has blessed him. He should take it upon himself to teach others, or to write on the subject. Similarly, someone who has a tendency to do acts of kindness, might find it particularly satisfying to establish a *chessed* project. By bringing out these abilities which are contained within and yearn to be realized, he will indeed feel Simchah and great satisfaction!

Perfection of Deed

At times a person is actively engaged in a mitzvah, job or project, but he is not fully satisfied. When this is the case, he should consider the possibility of modifying his initial, natural approach to the task at hand. By being willing to change *himself* to reach his goal more perfectly, he will grow and find greater satisfaction.

Let us take, as an example, an advanced Torah student. There are times when a *Ben Torah* is not completely satisfied with the quality of his studies. One of the Torah leaders of our generation offered one possible solution (*Miktavim U'Ma'amarim*): "This happens to them because they do not learn in the proper manner, [which would be] to learn *Gemara*, Rashi and Tosfot...[to understand thoroughly but] not to remain on each passage of the *Gemora* for days. Instead, [they must] always [be] learning further...and foremost, review.... I have no doubt that after he finishes the tractate, he will find satisfaction that he knows, in the course of a year, one, two, three or four tractates. *This* will cause him satisfaction! And if you listen to my advice, you will be happy; the Simchah will come."

We learn a great lesson from this: Studying Torah is the Jew's ultimate purpose, which certainly *can* bring one to the greatest Simchah. Still, if one merely goes according to his natural tendencies, doing what comes easiest, even in Torah, he can miss the opportunity to achieve the true potential for Simchah. We must be willing to check and modify ourselves to discover whatever method is most expedient for our *ultimate* ascent and growth.

Let's consider a housewife. Sometimes, instead of taking care of her children, she becomes preoccupied with her housework. She begins to feel deeply dissatisfied, for she feels that something is wrong. Perhaps she has confused her priorities and is not using good judgement. When this happens, *regardless* of her natural inclinaton, she should consider ignoring the appearance of the house and giving her children the love they long for. By being flexible and willing to modify herself she will grow in this area. In this way she will find true self-realization and Simchah.

Of course, the above are just two examples of life's countless occupations. But no matter what the task, the more a person is willing to pause and subject their natural tendencies to deeper consideration, in order to equip themselves to meet the challenge at hand, the more he will grow, and the more his Simchah will increase.

A Forced Situation

There are times when a person is *forced* to deal with matters that are, in his opinion, not his main destiny in life, and this causes him to be unhappy. He feels that he is not utilizing his abilities properly and is stagnating. When this occurs, it is wise for one to alter his way of thinking. After all, who said that his destiny must be exactly what he had anticipated? Perhaps he should change course and set new horizons for himself. In this way, he may begin to feel himself growing, perhaps even in that area in which he was initially so disappointed.

Sometimes, such a state of affairs is only temporary. Instead of necessitating a complete revision of thought, it requires only a revision of proportions. He should think to himself that the present situation is only temporary and does not really contradict his main destiny at all. There will be other times when he will be able to pursue his goals in accordance with his main abilities, with HaShem's help.

For example, a person is taking care of children or doing

some other type of *chessed* which seems irrelevant to his personal fulfillment and growth. He should relate to it as a temporary situation and search for the value in what he is doing. He should realize the value of *chessed* and of giving to others, as nothing G-d has given him is devoid of value — and this will make him happy.

Acquire a Friend

Another suggestion for rising above unhappiness to the state of Simchah is found in the letters of HaGaon Rav Yisroel Kanievsky, Ztz"l (*Etzot V'Hadrachot* 59b). He advises that one acquire a close friend. As the mutual feelings of love, trust and intimacy develop, other positive feelings will also unfold, and so, he will begin feeling more successful in life.

According to our theory, we can explain that the unhappy person is contained within himself, limited within his own boundaries. His aspirations are suppressed, his spirit is broken. He has no desire to become involved in new activities or associate himself with new things that are outside his own limits. But when a person develops a bond with someone other than himself, he *breaks through* the chains that bind him within his own periphery. Subsequently, his wishes and desires will come to life again, and he will aspire to realize them in practice. In the words of the psalmist, David: "...Out from the confinement to the expanse." Similarly, it is a good idea to speak to a friend and to open one's heart to him. The more a person reveals the concealed feelings within himself — his distress, his agony, and also his unhappiness — the more intense his

Simchah grows and the more his abilities develop in general, as he senses that his feelings are no longer confined within him.

The Power of Growth

Many a story is told about sick people who gave up hope, only to come out of their distress when they began to create, to act, and to do things. Every action and deed — even deeds that a person is not used to doing and does not consider as the main purpose of his life — brings Simchah.

A story about the *tzadeket*, Chedvah Zilberfarb, of blessed memory, illustrates this principle (from *Gesher Chedvah* p. 205):

> "The night fell, darkness was all around, not a star was shining on the horizon of her life. The disease was debilitating, the doctors almost lost all hope. Chedvah was in low spirits. It looked as though her strong will was about to yield. The people around her tried to give her encouragement, to imbue her with some new hope. But all the ideas and all the suggestions did not succeed in kindling a spark of life in her. Then suddenly, a close friend whose husband runs a department store, comes up with an idea. 'Why don't we go out together to choose some pretty socks for the kids?" Chedvah hears what her friend has suggested and a smile appears on her lips. She gets up quickly, sheds off the cloak of grief, and seems to forget the whole world.

Now she is going to buy for her children, to
bring happiness to the toddlers who are so
dear to her!"

How powerful is that act — "bringing happiness to the
toddlers who are so dear to her" — and bringing the sub-
merged will from the potential to the actual. This act is
what succeeded in freeing Chedvah from her mantle of
grief and distress. How great is the power of growth!

2

SIMCHAH VERSUS MOCKERY

Even though we learned that growing and expanding through Simchah is a positive Torah trait, not all types of Simchah are positive and constructive. In this chapter, we shall try to clarify the difference between Torah-oriented Simchah, on the one hand, and jesting and mockery on the other.

Let us examine a passage in the Torah which will enable us to reach a deeper understanding of the meaning of these two concepts. We learn (Bereshit 17:17):

> "Avraham fell upon his face and he laughed.
> He said in his heart: 'Shall [a child] be born to
> a hundred-year-old man, and shall Sarah, a
> ninety-year old woman, give birth?' "

Unkelos translates the word *veyitzchak* (he laughed), into the Aramaic *chadi* — "he was in Simchah."

Another verse (ibid., 18:12):

> "Sarah laughed within herself, saying, 'After
> I am waxed out, shall I be rejuvenated, my
> master being old also?' "

Here, Unkelos translates the same word, *vatizchak*, as *vechaychat*, which implies that Sarah scoffed in derision. Rashi adds that we can perceive from this that Avraham believed and was happy, while Sarah did not believe, and "laughed." As a result, *HaKadosh Baruch Hu* was stringent with Sarah but was lenient with Avraham.

From this scene, we can discern that there are two types of laughter. One expresses Simchah, and the other conveys mockery. The Torah includes these two categories of laughter in one term, *veyitzchak*, but in reality they are opposites. The laughter of Simchah reflects and affirms a person's belief in the authenticity of his faith. In his case, laughter expresses his appreciation of that truth: "Avraham believed and was happy." The second type of laughter displays a person's lack of belief because he relates to the subject as unrealistic: "Sarah did not believe, and sneered."

Now that we understand the two contradictory types of Simchah, we can proceed to consider the essence of the activity which we will call extreme laughter.

Laughter — the Inappropriate Opposite of Sadness

The Rambam (*Hilchot Deot* 2:7) writes: "One should not be a person who always laughs and jokes, nor should one be sad or melancholy, but happy. In the words of our Sages, 'Laughter and frivolity accustom a man to immorality.' "

Whereas sadness prevents a person from realizing his inner potential, laughter can cause a loosening of the barriers and prohibitions governing one's behavior, to the extent that one might come to actualize *all* his aspirations, including those which are undesirable, negative and destructive. Simchah, on the other hand, is the key to achieving the desired *balance* between laughter and sadness. A person who is filled with Simchah will actualize only the potential good within him and produce desirable and noble results in all of life's challenges.

Jesting and Mockery

The definition of extreme laughter is explained in the words of the Maharal (*Derech Chayim Avot* 6): "Exaggerated laughter is in contrast to thought, which is [a function of] the mind. There is no doubt that mockery and jesting are contrary to wisdom, because jesting has no substance other than farce, whereas the mind has true value. Laughter, therefore, repels the mind."

We learn from the Maharal that the power of exaggerated laughter — about which our Sages stated, "One mockery undoes a hundred rebukes" — erases the entire impression that words of wisdom and morality make on the listeners. This stems from the fact that laughter tends to ignore all boundaries. Once a person turns away from all limitations, he gives himself free license to unleash his negative thoughts, which can then produce destructive behavior.

We learn in the *Mishnah* (*Avot* 3:16): "Accept every person with Simchah;" but we also learn (ibid., 3:17): "Rabbi Akiva says, 'laughter and frivolity accustom a man to immorality.'" HaGaon Rav Yosef Yavetz explains that these two *mishnayot* were written one after another, to teach us that even though laughter and Simchah appear to be similar on the surface, they are actually diametrically opposed to one another. Whereas Simchah stems from the mind, the source of laughter is the lower, "animal soul."

The Secret of a Joke

We can now understand the pleasure that comes from hearing "a good joke." The joke is generally a story that is in opposition and contrast to the order and the rules of the world. When one hears a joke, he is encouraged to begin feeling that he, too, now has the freedom to laugh in the face of reality and to do *whatever* comes into his mind.

What if a prominent and respected professor were being honored with the Nobel Prize. Walking up to the stage, he slips on his open shoelace and falls flat on the ground. It is very difficult for the people witnessing this mishap to resist their urge to laugh. The appearance of a dignified man generally commands the respect of those around him, and his fall, which created a loss of dignity, brings a feeling of relief from the usual, restricting reality. Subsequently, laughter results.

A joke can be looked at as a bridge between mockery and true Simchah. The mechanics of a joke are similar to mockery in the sense that both create an impression of imaginary freedom and power. Used positively, however, a joke can truly enlighten the heart and bring it to a state of Simchah. Bearing this in mind, we can now travel to the other side of the bridge to understand the positive side of amusement.

3

AMUSEMENT AND PLEASURE

A Good-Humored State of Mind

Although we have learned that jesting and mockery are deplorable attributes that signify escape from reality, the "good-humored state of mind" (בדיחות הדעת) *is* a positive trait.

This virtue, which we might call "being amused", is mentioned in the *Gemara* (*Shabbat* 30b):

> "Before opening his lesson to his students, Rabbah would say a word of humor, and they were amused. Thereafter, he would sit down and solemnly begin the lesson."

Rashi comments: "Words of humor prior to the lecture are necessary in order to 'open the heart' through Simchah."

From this we learn that the state of being amused does not contradict the acquisition of Torah, as does mockery and jesting. On the contrary, it contributes to broadening a person's mind and to the ability to receive words of wisdom.

An example of this relationship is found in the words of
Rava, who said about himself (*Eruvin* 29a): "I am like Ben
Azai in the marketplace of Tiberias." Rashi explains: "It
was a day when Rava was in a good-humored mood, and
he said to his pupils, 'Now my mind is clear and I am
prepared to reply to anyone who will ask me a question —
like Ben Azai, to whom no one compared in "tearing out
mountains" (a talmudic expression implying genius and
sharpness of the mind in solving problems).' "

We learn, therefore, that when a person is in a good-humored state of mind, he is actually capable of acquiring
more knowledge and wisdom than usual.

The Definition of Being Amused

What is the definition of that proper amusement, or
"good-humored state," and how does it contribute to a
man's wisdom?

We find a description of this trait in *Alei Shur* (Vol. 2,
242):

> "This trait of having amusement of mind,
> popularly known as good humor, is a virtue
> which generates mercy on the unfortunate,
> forgiveness to the weak-minded, a sharp eye
> to the shortcomings of people without con-
> tempt for their dignity, the ability to rise
> above embarrassing situations, insight into
> the light within the negative and the negative
> within the light — [promoting a personality
> in which] cleverness and love are bound to-
> gether. A person who is in a humorous state
> always has a pleasant disposition and good

spirits....[The term 'humor'] is very far from joking and light-headedness, G-d forbid... 'Words of humor' [as Chazal understood the phrase,] does not mean what we call today joking and mocking. But they [Chazal] did enjoy the aforementioned kind of humor, that which brought those who were sad and those in conflict to see their problems in a more positive manner."

As an example of the state of being amused, we quote from what is told about the Torah prince, HaGaon Rav Chaim Shmulevitz, Ztz"l (*Moach VaLev*): "When he was learning, Rav Chaim would virtually *melt* with Simchah. A smile always hovered at the corner of his lips. Not withstanding his seriousness and tremendous concentration, he abounded with tireless excitement and energy. He used many different expressions of Simchah in the course of learning, some of which can only be appreciated in their original Yiddish. These expressions, witty and sharp plays on words, were infectious and would create a happy, alert atmosphere. Many of his comments about *sevorot* [talmudic reasonings] were full of incisive and lively humor. Concerning an acceptable insight, he would eloquently proclaim, 'It's sweeter than tar.' Concerning a point which had finally been clarified he would say, 'It's *sossondik*' or '*simchahdik*!' "

The Secret of Amusement

Defining the virtue of good-humoredness enables us to understand the secret of its power to uplift a person's spirit. Amusement is the connecting virtue between laughter and mockery. On the one hand, it does not ignore reality, while on the other, it alleviates a person's sadness and stimulates him to think more positively.

The type of humor which gives wisdom also works in this manner. In his usual state of mind, a person feels that he has limited mental capacities, meager wisdom and little ability to grasp things. The words of humor that the Sages used before beginning to teach Torah brought their students to a much higher level of comprehension, revealing inner resources far greater than they had realized. And in the words of the Baal Shem Tov (*Likutim*, Tractate *Shabbat*): "...bring a person out of 'littleness' to greatness."

Simchah through Physical Pleasures

Physical pleasure is another way to lift up one's spirit from sadness to Simchah. As long as the pleasure is a means and not an end in itself, the Torah considers it a positive activity.

Rabbeinu Yonah writes (*Sha'arei Teshuvah* 2:9):

> "Since an elderly person is not able to taste what he eats or drinks, *he should enjoy and appreciate* the sunlight and not cause anguish to himself. He should be joyous during all his years, in order not to lose any years of life, and he should never cease to serve G-d. The righteous become stronger in their old age; they prepare for battle and gather their strength to serve G-d, as the Sages say: 'When *talmidei chachamim* grow older, their wisdom in-

creases.' The verse says (Psalms 92:15): 'They
will still be fruitful in old age, vigorous and
fresh they will be, to declare that HaShem is
just....' "

It is evident from the above passage that it is not only
permissible to enjoy permitted forms of physical pleasure,
but that it is even considered an essential element in serving G-d. The pleasant sensation of warm sunlight on one's
skin or the sweet taste of a fruit has the effect of lifting
one's spirit, and creates a feeling of general well-being. Un-
questionably, mitzvot performed in this ambience are superior in quality to those performed in an air of
despondency.

This idea is discussed in the work, *Noam Elimelech*: "One
who wishes to subjugate the *kelipot* [the Forces of Evil in
the world] must remain in good spirits continuously. When
one is happy, it is impossible to be sad. Thus, when one
emotion wanes, the other rises in its stead. Although it
would be proper for a person, especially a righteous one, to
maintain a continuous state of selflessness and service to
G-d, HaShem sometimes causes a person to have specific
desires for certain things. He then allows those desires to
be fulfilled, for this causes the person to feel happy. This, in
turn, subjugates the *kelipot*. Even a person who is not on
such a high level can cause the *kelipot* to become subju-
gated, by simply enjoying physical pleasures and blessing
HaShem for them."

In fact, this concept is so central to Judaism that the
Sages incorporated it in the blessing which is recited after
eating fruit:

"Blessed are You, HaShem, our G-d, King of

the universe, Who creates numerous living things with their deficiencies; for all that You have created, with which to maintain the life of every being. Blessed is He, the Life of the worlds."

The classic legal codifier, the *Tur*, paraphrases the blessing as follows: "...Who creates numerous living things and that which they lack (such as food and water), and also all the other things in the world which are not essential for the survival of those living things (such as fruit)." The *Beit Yosef* explains on this that those foods which are not essential for man's survival were created in order to "maintain the life of every being, to revive the soul and to awaken the heart of man to happiness."

Conclusion

We see, then, that humor and physical pleasure are potent forces which lift the human spirit out of sadness and help a person develop an attitude of amusement. This state of good-humoredness, in turn, opens the heart and clarifies the mind. Although proper words of humor act in a way similar to laughter and mockery, by lifting the person out of his present state, a humorous state of mind does not imply ignoring or denying reality. On the contrary, it helps us to discover that reality is not always as it may seem, but should be looked upon more positively.

4

TYPES OF HAPPINESS

Considering that Simchah and growth are complementary and positive, while sadness and confinement are their negative counterparts, we may now understand the psychological dynamics behind the day-to-day activities which cause us to be happy. Happiness can be divided into two categories: happiness towards growth, and the happiness of accomplishment (during and upon achieving growth). Let us begin with the first category.

Happiness Towards Growth

Youthful Joy

In a Torah discourse, Rav Moshe Shapiro asked: "Why is a person happy when he wakes up in the morning? True, he wakes up rejuvenated and is no longer broody and moody. But what is it that *makes him happy*? And in the same vein, why, in general, are young people happy and the elderly sad?"

He answers, that first thing in the morning, all of one's

options seem open, the possibilities the new day presents seem promising and glorious, and everything seems potentially under one's control. One feels free and unlimited. By evening, however, these options no longer exist. One has done whatever he has done, achieved whatever he has achieved, and there is no more possibility of doing more or doing things differently.

Youth and old age are even stronger examples of this same progression. The young person revels in his potential, not in his accomplishments, while the old man mourns his lost potential, ignoring the value of his accomplishments now that he has little chance to increase them.

The housewife browsing through the aisles in the supermarket, selecting and comparing the products, in a way senses this youthful joy. The man shopping for a sophisticated electronic appliance, choosing between the latest models — he, too, is sparked with this same youthful happiness.

What is it in such situations and activities that brings about a joyous feeling? On the contrary, the long lines of people, the bother and the confusion that goes with choosing between the numerous products should cause difficulty and consternation.

The answer is, that the exposure to such an abundance of products fosters an imaginary sense that one possesses new vistas of growth, new possibilities. Even if, in the end, one buys the same product that one is used to, the very *possibility* of obtaining something new causes one this vibrant feeling of happiness.

Similarly, reading fiction and fantasy stories or hearing the news from far and unknown places also causes pleasure, for we imagine new worlds revealed before us, and we envision new possibilities.

TYPES OF HAPPINESS / 175

We must not altogether disqualify this type of happiness. At times, it is necessary to feel such a sense of renewal and rejuvenation. However, this happiness cannot be our life's objective. It is unreal and transient, made to vanish with time, like the passing happiness of one waking in the morning, or the youth's fresh joy which diminishes with each passing option.

Happiness over Accomplishment

But it is not always this illusionary, transient type of joy which leads us to feel happiness. There are times when our *true* dreams become reality, when we are happy over our actual accomplishments. Here too, however, the happiness can be subdivided into two types: Happiness over a real achievement of intrinsic value, and happiness over fantasies which have no lasting value. Let us begin by discussing the second type.

Happiness of Expansionism

Millions of people roar with satisfaction over the victory of a soccer team, till they lose their senses! How can we rationalize this enthusiasm, the ecstastic cheering of a throng of paying adults over the "achievement" of strangers kicking a ball into a net between two wooden poles?

At the end of Part One, we discussed the urge called "expansionism" which is often the source of happiness. This type of satisfaction stems from the urge to attain something beyond one's immediate control, even if the achievement may be only vicarious, fantastic and lacking any true substance. Man aspires to endless possibilities.

The force of inertia and the impulse of adventure motivate us to desire to attain *anything*, just because it is unattainable, without considering whether or not we really have any use for it. "Happiness" in the victory of one's soccer team is not over achieving anything of positive value, but rather, just a matter of *overcoming*, per se.

The pleasure people find in extravagant trips to faraway places is of much the same sort. The happiness in doing these things is actually the pleasure of attaining something *which was previously beyond one's grasp*, rather than in the obtained object itself. A man who succeeds in reaching the moon and conquering outer space has "expanded his horizons" in an extreme way, to the point of illusion: there is nothing beyond his reach.

The Question

Of course, expansionism is not the only motivation for everything new under the sun. Many innovations and achievements are of true value, to the benefit of mankind and the perfection of Creation. However, there are also the tens of thousands of dollars spent on unnecessary renovations, the hundreds of thousands spent on ill-considered college degrees, the thousands thrown out for fancy cars... clear footprints of the expansionist desire.

Now let us ask ourselves which kinds of happiness we ought to pursue and which we should minimize, or even give up.

It goes without saying that the most worthwhile Simchah is that of true achievements, whereas Simchah over accomplishments which are of no substance should be minimized. *Certainly* they should not become a life objective.

The question arises, then: Why do people not realize their mistake and recognize that their "happiness" is over things which have no value? Why do they not consider that empty happiness itself can have no value?

Endless Aspirations

The answer is that man is driven by an endless sequence of desires. As soon as he reaches one goal, he is already dreaming of the next one. Once again dissatisfied, he is again overcome by the fantasy that he will at last find happiness in realizing his new desires. If he would only stop a moment to consider the sum-total of his accomplishments, he would soon recognize that through this approach to life he has actually obtained little of value, and that little of what he has gained has actually brought him any lasting satisfaction.

There is a well-known story of one such *ba'al teshuvah*, who *literally* reached the heights of secular Israeli society...and was fortunate enough to have lived to tell the tale. He was a top fighter pilot, the most sought-after position in the Israeli army, and he truly felt superior to everyone around him. At the controls of his aircraft's modern, sophisticated systems, he felt at the height of power. Traveling throughout the world, he enjoyed all the physical pleasures a person could dream of, reveling in his status and success.

One day, however, when this young man had seemingly realized every dream and appeared to have reached the pinnacle of his life, he stopped. At that moment, his eyes found no other vista to conquer, and his drive for more *paused for a moment*. This moment was his moment of truth. Suddenly he found himself thinking about all his marvelous achievements, and for the first time he clearly saw that his life and career were essentially empty and meaningless. Now, with all doors open before him, he could suddenly see that none of them were worth walking through. The doors, as well as the rooms they led to, were like circus balloons: all glitter on the outside, but empty within (*Shey-lah U'Tshuvah* 119).

Conclusion

The lesson of the above story applies to *all of us*. Who is completely free of the pursuit of imaginary goals? Why should we wait until we reach the end of the road and only then recognize how meaningless was the goal we had been pursuing? Instead, let us stop right now and look around to see where we are heading. In this way we can hope to attain the complete Simchah: the Simchah that begins when we first dream of the goal, continues while pursuing the goal, and does not terminate after having reached that goal — the Simchah of eternity.

5

THE ULTIMATE SIMCHAH

Now that we have defined the different types of happiness, we are prepared to discuss and comprehend the ultimate Simchah — *Simchah in mitzvot* and *Simchah in HaShem*.

On the surface, it may appear that one who leads a carefree life, unhampered by laws and regulations, is a happy person, while someone who is limited by the precepts and laws of the Torah must be unfortunate and sad. This erroneous evaluation is based on the assumption that a person is happier when he manages to fulfill his every desire, fulfilling his wishes unchecked, compared to one who subjects himself to rules and obeys commandments, curbing his satisfactions and compromising his wishes. However, if we look into the matter more deeply, we discover that the truth is quite the opposite. True eternal Simchah is found specifically among the Servants of HaShem.

One of the foremost ethical masters, Reb Yosef Yoizel Hurwitz, Ztz"l, once remarked (*Tenuat HaMussar*, Vol. 4, 349): "In my life I knew only one person who was really happy. It was Reb Yisroel Salanter!" This is indeed remarkable: the elder Reb Yoizel had met many people in his life, yet he never saw a truly happy man other than Reb Yis-roel? Furthermore, Reb Yisroel, Ztz"l, had been preoccu-pied all his life with the virtue of *Yirah* (awe and reverence of HaShem), constantly fighting his Evil Inclination and conquering his temptations. Certainly one would think that these preoccupations run contrary to leading a life of Sim-chah! So let us try to understand the secret of Simchah in mitzvot.

Earlier, we learned that the source of Simchah is growth. Of course, a person is eager to fulfill his material desires, and on the surface, it seems that this kind of "growth" would bring him happiness. However, if we look into the depths of his soul, we will discover that it is not so.

The task of a person in life is actually to fulfill his duty to HaShem, through His Torah, His laws and His mitzvot. Through the performance of mitzvot, man comes close to his Creator, the source of his soul. Every person was given the spiritual and psychological power to fulfill his destiny, but we each also possess certain negative tendencies. The ultimate task in a person's life is to curb these inner "nega-tive forces", to overcome them, and to draw only on the positive ones instead. Consciously and unconsciously, in the depths of our souls beats the profound desire to fulfill our destiny — to acquire spiritual perfection, the ultimate growth. In the words of Rav Alexandri (*Berachot* 17b): "'Our will is to do Your will.' Who, then, is in the way? The 'leaven in the dough' [the Evil Inclination] and the servi-tude to the [foreign] kingdoms [influence of foreign val-ues]."

Ancient Greek philosophers as well as modern psycholo-gists have all reached the same conclusion: One of the most profound and overriding desires of man is to attain perfection. The source of this yearning is the soul which HaShem breathed into our nostrils, that which, by its nature, longs to return to its Source, the Creator, through performing mitzvot and rising to higher spheres of spiritual perfection. We learn from the Rambam (*Hilchot Gerushin* 2:20):

> "When one is obligated by the law to divorce his wife and he refuses to do so, a Jewish court pressures him until he says: 'I am willing.' The *get* [divorce document] that he writes is valid."

[The Rambam goes on to explain why this is considered a valid *get*, although it was given without consent:]

> "Whoever is influenced by his Evil Inclination to transgress a mitzvah or to commit a sin, and who is then physically coerced until he does what he was obligated to do, or until he refrained from what was forbidden, this does not indicate that he was compelled to do so unwillingly. Rather, his [previous] refusal resulted from having forced himself through his "Evil Inclination" to go against his [inner, good] will. Therefore, a person who refuses to give a *get*, —since he really wants to be part of the Jewish community and [subconsciously] aspires to observe all the mitzvot and refrain from sin, yet is compelled by his Evil Inclination to do otherwise — now that he has been harassed until his Evil Inclination has weakened and he said, "I am willing," it is considered that he gave the *get* willingly."

Thus, we learn from the Rambam that it is actually the innate inner will of every Jew to do the will of HaShem. Like an ecstatic baby taking his first tentative steps, setting into motion the limitless forces contained within himself, so is a Jew's joy when he merits to live a meaningful life and realize his spiritual potential. He experiences great joy precisely *because* he is successful in resisting all types of temptation with which he is confronted.

In his commentary on *Pirkei Avot* (4:4), the Rambam relates: "I read in one of the classic books dealing with character development about a prominent, pious man who was asked to relate *the happiest experience* of his life. He answered that on one of his travels on board a ship, he did not have a proper resting place and he had to rest between the cargo packages. On board were some well-to-do merchants. One of them got up and went over to the corner where this pious man was lying. He appeared despicable in the eyes of the arrogant merchant, to the extent that the merchant humiliated the pious man in a disgusting manner. 'I swear by G-d that my soul was not hurt by his deed at all, and my pride within me did not rebel,' said the pious man, 'and I was *very* happy that the humiliation at the hand of that merchant did not cause me anguish.' This is, no doubt, the ultimate humility of the mind," concludes the Rambam.

Victory over the desire for pride and the curbing of one's desires, as we see, leads to utmost happiness.

The Truly Happy Life

The assumption of many Jews throughout the generations, (such as was demonstrated by the Enlightenment movement) that happiness is to be found in a carefree, hedonistic or simply secular lifestyle, has led people to forsake the ways of Torah and abandon their unique heritage. Foolishly, they chose to follow their non-Jewish neighbors, rationalizing that freedom from the yoke of Torah and mitzvot would guarantee a much greater share of happiness. Yet in our own generation, we witness among many such assimilated Jews a pressing need to search through the embers of their spiritual identity in order to once more discover their roots and integrate the wisdom and teachings of our Torah.

In *Sefer She'eylah U'Tshuvah* (p. 132), a *ba'al teshuvah* who had attained all the pleasures of this world testifies: "I experienced an overwhelming feeling that my life was empty. I understood that such a life does not contribute to the growth of a man, and that his destiny cannot come to fruition."

Similarly, another *ba'al teshuvah* relates: "I was learning Hebrew in an Ulpan, and the teacher read to us from several Hebrew texts. Among these were some proverbs of wisdom from the *Pirkei Avot* . The first one happened to be: 'Who is a hero? He who conquers his *yetzer* (will).' This was a startling discovery. For a long time I had been analyzing the characters of heroes in European literature. The peak of their heroism lies in the frenzy of their passions, in the voluptuous pursuit of life's pleasures, and in submitting themselves to the indulgence of all their basest desires. Here, in one sentence, I was introduced to a character trait that stands in absolute contrast to the accepted world's hero. The hero of Judaism is one who conquers his will, curbs it, defeats it, directs it and leads it to do good and benevolent deeds. He triumphs over the negative and the evil in the *yetzer*. I felt that I, as one who was well-versed in European culture, could perceive the depths of this moral teaching, and for this alone, I can proclaim, 'You have chosen us from all nations.' "

The truth of the teachings of Torah opened the eyes of this literary critic, and made him aware of his mistake. It enabled him to differentiate between the void and darkness of European culture and the richness and light of the Torah of Israel.

Conclusion

We have learned that one who performs mitzvot discovers and revels in the ultimate happiness. The more a person succeeds in achieving the goal for which his soul longs — to come closer to his Creator — the happier he is. "Be glad in HaShem, rejoice, you righteous, and shout for joy, all you who are upright in heart" (Psalms 33:11).

Summary of the Book

The pursuit of happiness is a universal quest. This in-depth analysis sheds light on how true happiness can be achieved. We have seen that the Torah actually commands us to pursue happiness, and even paves the way to achieving it. Our Sages have taught us how to internalize the virtue of Simchah. Reviewing and applying their teachings, as quoted in this book, will surely help a person lead a life of happiness and contentment — *Passive Simchah*. Finally, HaShem in His Torah composed a network of mitzvot which fills life with endless vistas of spiritual perfection — the source of *Active Simchah*, for Simchah is produced by growth and accomplishment. How privileged is a person who fills his life with true values — the source of the Simchah of eternity!

GLOSSARY

Torah and N'viim

Devarim: Deuteronomy
Divrei HaYamim: Chronicles
Iyov: Job
Kohelet: Ecclesiastes
Mishlei: Proverbs
Shir HaShirim: Song of Songs
Tehillim: Psalms
Yeshayah: Isaiah

Other Words

Berachah: blessing
Chesed: goodness
Gemara: the Aramaic portion of the Talmud
Gematria: numerical value of the Hebrew letters
HaKadosh Baruch Hu: G-d
Halachah: traditional law
HaShem: G-d
Kabbalah: Jewish mysticism
Mitzvah: deed of merit
Mitzvot: deeds of merit
Motzoei: the night following the holiday
Mussar: Jewish ethics
Posek: a Rav who gives halachic decisions
Shlita: he should live a long and blessed life
Yetzer Hora: evil inclination
Yom Tov: Holiday

לעילוי נשמת

This book is dedicated
in loving memory of our dear aunt

ברכה בת ר' אריה לייב ע"ה

ע"ה **BERTHA ISRAEL**

whose love and concern
will remain in our hearts forever

נלב"ע שביעי של פסח תשנ"ה

ת.נ.צ.ב.ה.

In loving memory:

Revered father

ELYAHU BEN JACOB COHEN

Man of integrity and devotion

Beloved sister

SARA BAT SHALOM AND GULIA HAYUN

Devoted mother, teacher of religious and moral values, woman of Chessed and helper of the helpless

God bless their souls, amen

Sonny (Ben-Zion) Kahn
Miami Beach Florida

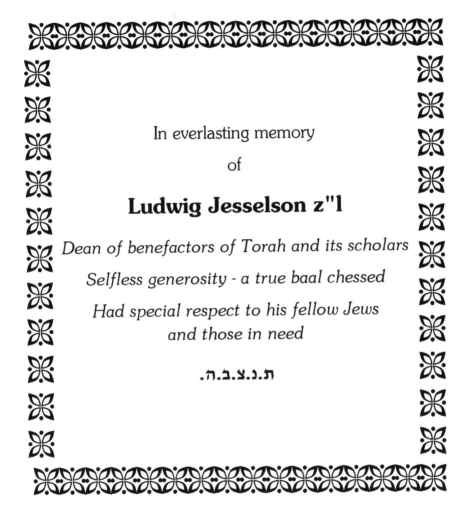

In everlasting memory

of

Ludwig Jesselson z"l

Dean of benefactors of Torah and its scholars

Selfless generosity - a true baal chessed

*Had special respect to his fellow Jews
and those in need*

.ת.נ.צ.ב.ה

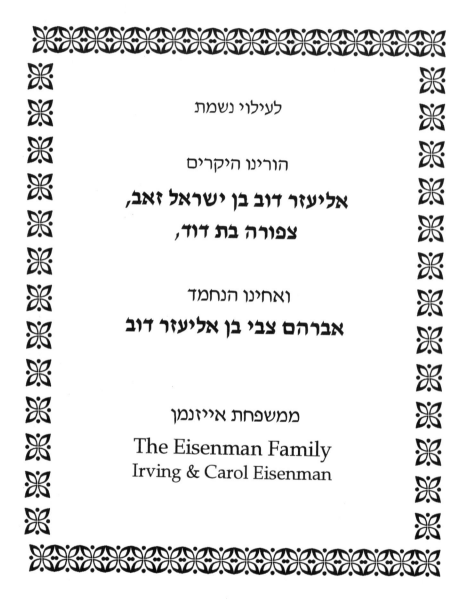

לעילוי נשמת

הורינו היקרים

אליעזר דוב בן ישראל זאב,

צפורה בת דוד,

ואחינו הנחמד

אברהם צבי בן אליעזר דוב

ממשפחת אייזנמן

The Eisenman Family

Irving & Carol Eisenman